The Ultimate Casserole Cookbook

Dishes, Volume 12

Olivia Bennett

Published by B&H Publishing Group, 2025.

THE ULTIMATE CASSEROLE COOKBOOK

First edition. February 24, 2025.

ISBN: 979-8227143990

Written by Olivia Bennett.

Table of Contents

To the home cooks who find joy in layering flavors,

to the busy parents seeking comfort in a one-dish meal,

and to everyone who believes that food brings people together.

May your kitchen be filled with warmth, laughter, and the delicious
aroma of a casserole baking in the oven.

This book is for you.

Introduction: The World of Casseroles

Casseroles are more than just a dish; they represent comfort, community, and culinary creativity. From their humble beginnings as a practical way to feed families to their current role as a versatile staple in kitchens around the world, casseroles have evolved into a beloved category of cooking. This chapter explores the history of casseroles, their enduring appeal for every occasion, and the essential tools and ingredients you need to create delicious, successful dishes every time.

The History of Casseroles

1. Ancient Roots

The concept of the casserole—combining ingredients in a single vessel and baking them—dates back thousands of years. While the word "casserole" comes from the French term for a deep, round dish, similar techniques were used in ancient cultures:

   - Greek and Roman Influence: Early cooks layered meats, grains, and vegetables in clay pots and baked them over open fires.

   - Middle Eastern Origins: Dishes like moussaka and pilaf utilized similar layering techniques, reflecting the shared traditions of baked, one-dish meals.

2. Medieval and Renaissance Developments

During the Middle Ages, pies and puddings dominated European cuisine, often serving as precursors to casseroles. The concept of layering ingredients—such as meat, root vegetables, and grains—became more refined. By the Renaissance, advances in baking technology allowed for better heat control, making baked dishes more common.

3. The Birth of the Modern Casserole

The modern casserole as we know it began to take shape in the 19th century, coinciding with innovations in cookware and ovens. Key developments included:

- Ceramic and Glassware: The creation of durable, heatproof baking dishes made casseroles more accessible.

- Canned Ingredients: In the early 20th century, the rise of convenience foods, such as canned soups and vegetables, revolutionized casserole cooking.

4. Casseroles in the Mid-20th Century

The 1950s and 1960s were the golden age of casseroles in America. Post-war households embraced them for their:

- Convenience: Perfect for busy families and working parents.

- Economy: A cost-effective way to feed a crowd.

- Creativity: Home cooks experimented with everything from Tuna Noodle Casserole to Jell-O molds.

5. Global Variations

Today, casseroles continue to evolve, influenced by diverse cuisines. Examples include:

- Lasagna: A classic Italian layered dish with pasta, cheese, and sauce.

- Shepherd's Pie: A British favorite made with meat and mashed potatoes.

- Tamale Pie: A Southwestern casserole featuring cornbread and spiced fillings.

Why Casseroles Are the Perfect Choice

Casseroles have maintained their popularity for a simple reason: they are versatile, convenient, and endlessly adaptable. Here are some of the reasons why casseroles remain a favorite in kitchens worldwide.

1. Simplicity

Casseroles are straightforward to prepare, making them ideal for cooks of all skill levels:

- Combine ingredients in one dish, bake, and serve.

- Minimal steps reduce the likelihood of mistakes, even for beginners.

2. Convenience

Busy lifestyles demand meals that are:

- Quick to Assemble: Many casseroles require just a few minutes of prep time.

- Make-Ahead Friendly: They can be prepared in advance, frozen, or refrigerated until needed.

- Easy to Serve: A casserole goes straight from oven to table, minimizing cleanup.

3. Endless Variety

The versatility of casseroles ensures there's something for everyone:

- Dietary Flexibility: Adapt recipes for vegetarian, vegan, low-carb, or gluten-free diets.

- Seasonal Ingredients: Use fresh produce for spring and summer casseroles or hearty root vegetables for autumn and winter.

- Flavor Profiles: Incorporate global influences like Mediterranean spices, Asian sauces, or Latin American heat.

4. Crowd-Pleasing Appeal

Casseroles are perfect for feeding groups:

- Serve as a centerpiece for potlucks, family dinners, and holidays.

- Easy to portion and customize for different preferences.

5. Comfort Factor

Few dishes evoke the warmth and nostalgia of a bubbling casserole straight from the oven:

- Cheesy Layers: Think mac and cheese or lasagna.

- Savory Fillings: Chicken pot pie or beef and potato bake.

- Sweet Indulgence: Desserts like bread pudding or peach cobbler casserole.

Essential Tools for Successful Casserole Cooking

1. Casserole Dishes

Invest in high-quality baking dishes to ensure even cooking and easy cleanup:

- Materials: Glass, ceramic, and cast iron retain heat well.

- Sizes: Standard sizes include 9x13 inches for larger casseroles and smaller dishes for individual portions.

2. Utensils

Equip your kitchen with versatile tools:

- Mixing Bowls: For combining ingredients.

- Spatulas and Spoons: For stirring and spreading.

- Ladles: For layering sauces or batters.

3. Measuring Tools

Precision is key in achieving perfect ratios:

- Measuring Cups and Spoons: For both dry and liquid ingredients.

- Kitchen Scale: Ideal for weighing ingredients like cheese or meat.

4. Knives and Cutting Boards

Sharp knives and durable cutting boards make prepping vegetables, proteins, and garnishes easier.

5. Aluminum Foil and Lids

Covering casseroles during baking helps:

- Prevent over-browning.

- Retain moisture for tender, juicy results.

Essential Ingredients for Casserole Success

1. Base Components

Every casserole needs a foundation:

- Grains: Rice, pasta, quinoa, or potatoes.

- Proteins: Chicken, beef, tofu, or beans.

- Vegetables: Fresh, frozen, or canned options.

2. Binding Agents

Hold the casserole together with creamy or saucy elements:

- Cheese: Shredded, sliced, or melted.

- Cream Soups: Mushroom, chicken, or celery varieties.

- Sauces: Marinara, béchamel, or curry-based.

3. Toppings

The perfect topping adds flavor and texture:

- Crumbs: Breadcrumbs, crushed crackers, or fried onions.
- Cheese: A golden, bubbly layer of cheddar, mozzarella, or Parmesan.
- Fresh Herbs: Parsley, basil, or cilantro for a vibrant finish.

4. Seasonings

Enhance flavors with a mix of spices and herbs:

- Classic: Salt, pepper, garlic, and onion powder.
- Bold: Smoked paprika, cumin, or red pepper flakes.
- Fresh: Rosemary, thyme, or dill.

Tips for Casserole Success

1. Layer Strategically

Layering affects both flavor distribution and cooking time:

- Place denser ingredients like grains or raw vegetables at the bottom.
- Spread sauces evenly to ensure moisture throughout the dish.

2. Don't Skimp on Seasoning

Casseroles can taste bland without adequate seasoning. Season each layer as you assemble the dish.

3. Mind the Cooking Time

Casseroles cook differently depending on their ingredients:

- Check for doneness by inserting a knife to ensure proteins are fully cooked and grains are tender.
- Avoid overbaking to prevent dryness.

4. Rest Before Serving

Letting casseroles rest for 5–10 minutes after baking allows the flavors to meld and makes slicing easier.

Conclusion

Casseroles are the epitome of comfort and versatility, offering endless possibilities for every cook and occasion. Their rich history, global appeal, and practical advantages make them a staple in kitchens around the world. With the right tools, ingredients, and techniques, anyone can create satisfying, memorable casseroles that bring people together and stand the test of time.

Whether you're a novice or a seasoned cook, the art of casserole-making is one that invites exploration, experimentation, and above all, enjoyment.

Chapter 1: Classic Casseroles

Casseroles are the ultimate comfort food, and classic casseroles hold a special place in culinary history. These dishes are rooted in tradition, evoking memories of family gatherings, potluck dinners, and hearty meals shared around the table. This chapter explores three timeless casserole recipes—Tuna Noodle Casserole, Chicken and Rice Bake, and Shepherd's Pie—along with tips for modernizing these classics without losing their nostalgic charm.

The Allure of Classic Casseroles

1. Why Classics Endure

Classic casseroles are more than just recipes; they are traditions passed down through generations. Their enduring popularity comes from:

- Simplicity: These dishes are easy to prepare, requiring minimal equipment and ingredients.

- Versatility: They can be adapted to suit different tastes and dietary needs.

- Comfort: Familiar flavors and hearty textures make them a go-to for cold nights or when craving something nostalgic.

2. Cultural Impact

Many classic casseroles have cultural significance, reflecting the flavors and cooking techniques of their origins:

- Shepherd's Pie: A staple of British cuisine, originally made to use up leftovers.

- Tuna Noodle Casserole: A mid-20th-century American invention born from convenience foods like canned soup and pasta.

- Chicken and Rice Bake: Found in cuisines worldwide, showcasing the universal appeal of this simple combination.

Recipe 1: Tuna Noodle Casserole

Tuna Noodle Casserole is a quintessential comfort dish that became a household staple in post-war America. It's an economical, hearty, and satisfying one-dish meal.

Ingredients:

- 12 oz egg noodles
- 2 cans (5 oz each) tuna, drained
- 1 can (10.5 oz) condensed cream of mushroom soup
- 1 cup milk
- 1 cup frozen peas
- 1 cup shredded cheddar cheese
- 1/2 cup crushed potato chips or breadcrumbs (for topping)
- 1/2 teaspoon garlic powder
- 1/2 teaspoon onion powder
- Salt and pepper to taste

Instructions:

1. Preheat oven to 375°F (190°C). Grease a 9x13-inch baking dish.

2. Cook egg noodles according to package instructions. Drain and set aside.

3. In a large mixing bowl, combine tuna, cream of mushroom soup, milk, peas, garlic powder, onion powder, and half of the cheese. Stir until well mixed.

4. Add the cooked noodles to the mixture and gently toss to coat.

5. Pour the mixture into the prepared baking dish. Top with the remaining cheese and sprinkle with crushed potato chips or breadcrumbs.

6. Bake for 20–25 minutes, or until the top is golden and bubbly. Serve hot.

Modernizing Tuna Noodle Casserole

- Healthier Version: Replace cream of mushroom soup with a homemade béchamel sauce using low-fat milk.

- Gourmet Touch: Use fresh tuna steaks instead of canned tuna, and swap cheddar for gruyere or parmesan.

- Add Vegetables: Incorporate sautéed mushrooms, diced carrots, or spinach for extra nutrients and flavor.

Recipe 2: Chicken and Rice Bake

Chicken and Rice Bake is a versatile dish that combines tender chicken, creamy rice, and aromatic seasonings. It's a staple in many households due to its simplicity and adaptability.

Ingredients:

- 4 bone-in, skin-on chicken thighs
- 1 cup long-grain rice
- 2 cups chicken broth
- 1 can (10.5 oz) cream of chicken soup
- 1 small onion, finely chopped
- 1 teaspoon garlic powder
- 1 teaspoon paprika
- 1/2 teaspoon dried thyme
- Salt and pepper to taste
- Fresh parsley for garnish

Instructions:

1. Preheat oven to 375°F (190°C). Grease a 9x13-inch baking dish.

2. In a large mixing bowl, combine rice, chicken broth, cream of chicken soup, onion, garlic powder, paprika, thyme, salt, and pepper. Mix well and pour into the baking dish.

3. Arrange chicken thighs on top of the rice mixture, skin-side up. Sprinkle with additional paprika for color.

4. Cover the dish tightly with aluminum foil and bake for 40 minutes.

5. Remove foil and bake for an additional 20 minutes, or until the chicken skin is crispy and the rice is fully cooked.

6. Garnish with fresh parsley and serve hot.

Modernizing Chicken and Rice Bake

- Healthier Version: Use brown rice or quinoa for added fiber, and replace cream of chicken soup with a yogurt-based sauce.

- Global Flavors: Add curry powder, coconut milk, and ginger for an Indian-inspired twist, or soy sauce, sesame oil, and green onions for an Asian flair.

- Vegetarian Option: Replace chicken with roasted vegetables like sweet potatoes, zucchini, and bell peppers.

Recipe 3: Shepherd's Pie

Shepherd's Pie is a classic British casserole made with ground meat and vegetables, topped with creamy mashed potatoes. Traditionally, lamb is used, but beef is a common substitute.

Ingredients:
- 1 lb ground lamb or beef
- 1 small onion, diced
- 2 carrots, diced
- 1/2 cup frozen peas
- 2 tablespoons tomato paste
- 1 tablespoon Worcestershire sauce
- 1 cup beef or vegetable broth
- 1 tablespoon all-purpose flour
- 4 cups mashed potatoes
- 1/2 cup shredded cheddar cheese (optional)
- Salt and pepper to taste

Instructions:

1. Preheat oven to 400°F (200°C).

2. In a large skillet, cook ground lamb or beef over medium heat until browned. Drain excess fat.

3. Add onion and carrots to the skillet. Cook until softened, about 5 minutes.

4. Stir in tomato paste, Worcestershire sauce, flour, and broth. Simmer until thickened. Add peas and season with salt and pepper.

5. Spread the meat mixture evenly in a baking dish. Top with mashed potatoes, spreading evenly with a spatula. Sprinkle with cheese if desired.

6. Bake for 20–25 minutes, or until the top is golden brown. Serve hot.

Modernizing Shepherd's Pie

- Healthier Version: Use ground turkey or plant-based meat, and top with mashed cauliflower instead of potatoes.

- Flavor Enhancements: Add red wine or fresh herbs like rosemary and thyme to the meat mixture for depth.

- Global Variations: Incorporate spices like cumin and coriander for a Middle Eastern twist, or add jalapeños and cheddar for a Tex-Mex version.

Tips for Perfecting Classic Casseroles

1. Balance Textures

- Use toppings like breadcrumbs or cheese to add crunch to creamy casseroles.

- Include fresh vegetables or herbs for a burst of color and texture.

2. Adjust Cooking Times

- Cook denser ingredients like raw vegetables or whole grains partially before adding them to the casserole.

- Ensure proteins like chicken or beef are fully cooked and tender.

3. Customize Portions

- Divide casseroles into individual ramekins for portion control and elegant presentation.

- Freeze portions for easy, ready-made meals during busy weeks.

4. Experiment with Layers

- Layer flavors strategically: start with grains or pasta, add a protein layer, then finish with sauce and toppings.

- Incorporate contrasting colors for visual appeal.

Conclusion

Classic casseroles like Tuna Noodle Casserole, Chicken and Rice Bake, and Shepherd's Pie have earned their place at the heart of home cooking. These recipes are comforting, versatile, and endlessly adaptable, making them ideal for any occasion. By understanding their traditional roots and exploring modern updates, you can breathe new life into these beloved dishes while honoring their nostalgic appeal. So preheat your oven, gather your ingredients, and enjoy the timeless joy of cooking and sharing classic casseroles.

Chapter 2: One-Dish Wonders for Busy Weeknights

Life is often hectic, and weeknights can feel like a race against the clock. After a long day, the last thing most people want to do is spend hours in the kitchen juggling multiple pots and pans. That's where one-dish casseroles shine. These versatile meals are quick, easy, and designed to save time while still delivering hearty, satisfying flavors. This chapter explores the art of crafting one-dish wonders perfect for busy weeknights, featuring recipes for Taco Casserole, Spinach and Mushroom Lasagna, and Cheeseburger Casserole. Plus, you'll learn time-saving prep tips and tricks to minimize cleanup.

Why One-Dish Meals Are Perfect for Weeknights

1. Convenience
   - Minimal Effort: Everything cooks in one dish, reducing the need for multiple pots and pans.
   - Streamlined Process: Simplified steps allow even novice cooks to succeed.
   2. Time-Saving
   - Quick Prep: Most recipes require only 15–20 minutes of active preparation.
   - Hands-Free Cooking: Once in the oven, casseroles cook themselves, giving you time to relax or multitask.
   3. Balanced Meals
   - Casseroles combine proteins, grains, and vegetables into a single dish, offering a complete meal with minimal fuss.
   4. Minimal Cleanup
   - Using one dish means fewer utensils and pans to wash, making post-dinner cleanup a breeze.

Recipe 1: Taco Casserole

Taco Casserole is a bold, flavorful dish that captures the essence of taco night without the mess of assembling individual tacos. It's a crowd-pleaser that's easy to customize with your favorite toppings.

Ingredients:
- 1 lb ground beef or turkey
- 1 packet taco seasoning
- 1 can (15 oz) black beans, drained and rinsed
- 1 cup frozen corn
- 1 cup salsa
- 2 cups tortilla chips, crushed
- 1 cup shredded cheddar cheese
- 1 cup shredded lettuce (for serving)
- 1 diced tomato (for serving)
- Sour cream and guacamole (optional, for serving)

Instructions:
1. Preheat oven to 375°F (190°C). Grease a 9x13-inch baking dish.

2. In a skillet over medium heat, cook the ground beef or turkey until browned. Drain excess fat and stir in taco seasoning according to the package instructions.

3. Add black beans, corn, and salsa to the skillet. Mix until well combined.

4. Layer half the crushed tortilla chips in the bottom of the baking dish. Spread the meat mixture evenly over the chips.

5. Top with the remaining tortilla chips and sprinkle shredded cheddar cheese over the top.

6. Bake for 15–20 minutes, or until the cheese is melted and bubbly.

7. Serve warm with shredded lettuce, diced tomatoes, sour cream, and guacamole on the side.

Tips:
- Use ground chicken or a plant-based meat alternative for a healthier option.

- Add diced jalapeños or hot sauce for extra spice.

Recipe 2: Spinach and Mushroom Lasagna

This vegetarian lasagna is a creamy, cheesy delight packed with earthy mushrooms and nutrient-rich spinach. It's a lighter option that doesn't skimp on flavor, perfect for Meatless Mondays or anytime you want a wholesome dish.

Ingredients:
- 9 lasagna noodles
- 2 tablespoons olive oil
- 1 lb mushrooms, sliced
- 3 cups fresh spinach
- 2 cups ricotta cheese
- 2 cups shredded mozzarella cheese
- 1 cup grated Parmesan cheese
- 1 jar (24 oz) marinara sauce
- 1 teaspoon garlic powder
- 1 teaspoon dried oregano
- Salt and pepper to taste

Instructions:

1. Preheat oven to 375°F (190°C). Grease a 9x13-inch baking dish.

2. Cook lasagna noodles according to package instructions. Drain and set aside.

3. In a skillet, heat olive oil over medium heat. Sauté mushrooms until softened, about 5 minutes. Add spinach and cook until wilted. Season with garlic powder, oregano, salt, and pepper. Remove from heat.

4. In a mixing bowl, combine ricotta cheese and half of the Parmesan cheese.

5. Spread a thin layer of marinara sauce on the bottom of the baking dish. Layer three lasagna noodles on top.

6. Spread one-third of the ricotta mixture over the noodles, followed by one-third of the mushroom and spinach mixture, a layer of marinara sauce, and a sprinkle of mozzarella cheese. Repeat layers twice more, ending with marinara and mozzarella on top.

7. Sprinkle the remaining Parmesan cheese over the casserole. Cover with aluminum foil and bake for 25 minutes. Remove foil and bake for an additional 10 minutes, or until the cheese is golden and bubbly.

8. Let rest for 10 minutes before serving.

Tips:
- Substitute zucchini slices for lasagna noodles to make it low-carb.
- Add red pepper flakes for a subtle kick.

Recipe 3: Cheeseburger Casserole

This fun, family-friendly casserole combines the flavors of a classic cheeseburger into a creamy, cheesy dish. It's a guaranteed hit with both kids and adults.

Ingredients:
- 1 lb ground beef
- 1 small onion, diced
- 1 teaspoon garlic powder
- 1 can (14.5 oz) diced tomatoes, undrained
- 1 cup ketchup
- 2 tablespoons mustard
- 2 cups cooked elbow macaroni
- 2 cups shredded cheddar cheese
- 1/4 cup pickles, chopped (optional, for garnish)

Instructions:
1. Preheat oven to 375°F (190°C). Grease a 9x13-inch baking dish.
2. In a skillet, cook ground beef and onion over medium heat until browned. Drain excess fat and stir in garlic powder, diced tomatoes, ketchup, and mustard. Simmer for 5 minutes.
3. Mix the cooked macaroni into the beef mixture. Transfer to the prepared baking dish.
4. Sprinkle shredded cheddar cheese evenly over the top.
5. Bake for 20 minutes, or until the cheese is melted and bubbly.
6. Garnish with chopped pickles if desired and serve warm.

Tips:
- Add crumbled bacon for a smoky twist.
- Use gluten-free pasta to accommodate dietary needs.

How to Prep Ahead and Minimize Cleanup

1. Time-Saving Prep Tips

- Chop Ahead: Pre-cut vegetables and store them in airtight containers in the refrigerator.

- Cook in Bulk: Prepare proteins like ground beef or shredded chicken in advance and freeze in portions.

- Assemble Early: Layer casseroles the night before and refrigerate. Bake them fresh the next day.

2. Smart Tools for Cleanup

- Use Disposable Pans: Great for potlucks or busy nights when you want to skip dishwashing.

- Line with Foil or Parchment: Makes cleanup faster by preventing baked-on messes.

- Dishwasher-Safe Utensils: Choose mixing bowls, spatulas, and knives that can go straight into the dishwasher.

3. Optimize Storage

- Divide leftovers into single-serving containers for easy reheating.

- Freeze portions for future meals, ensuring you always have something homemade on hand.

Tips for Making One-Dish Wonders Even Easier

1. Versatile Bases: Keep staples like pasta, rice, and canned beans in your pantry for quick casseroles.

2. Frozen Vegetables: These save prep time and work just as well as fresh ones in most recipes.

3. Double Recipes: Make extra and freeze half for another night.

4. Batch Cooking: Prepare multiple casseroles at once and freeze them for busy weeks.

Conclusion

One-dish casseroles are the ultimate solution for busy weeknights, offering a perfect balance of flavor, convenience, and minimal cleanup. Recipes like Taco Casserole, Spinach and Mushroom Lasagna, and Cheeseburger Casserole bring variety to your dinner table while requiring only a fraction of the effort compared to traditional multi-dish meals. By prepping ahead and following time-saving tips, you'll have more time to relax and enjoy your evenings, all while serving delicious, hearty meals that everyone will love.

Chapter 3: Breakfast and Brunch Casseroles

There's something magical about breakfast and brunch casseroles. They bring people together, whether it's for a holiday morning, a weekend brunch, or simply meal prepping for a busy week. These hearty, versatile dishes are easy to prepare, serve, and adapt to a variety of tastes. From savory options like Sausage and Egg Breakfast Bake to sweet indulgences like French Toast Casserole, breakfast casseroles can satisfy every palate. This chapter dives into recipes, tips, and variations to help you create memorable morning meals.

The Appeal of Breakfast and Brunch Casseroles

1. Perfect for Feeding a Crowd

- Easy to Scale: Most breakfast casseroles can be doubled or tripled to feed large groups.

- One-Dish Convenience: Serve straight from the oven, minimizing the need for multiple pans or serving dishes.

2. Ideal for Meal Prep

- Make Ahead: Assemble the night before and bake in the morning.

- Reheats Well: Many casseroles taste just as good, if not better, the next day.

3. Versatile Flavors

- Sweet or Savory: From cheesy eggs to caramelized French toast, there's a casserole for everyone.

- Customizable: Add or swap ingredients to accommodate dietary preferences and seasonal produce.

Recipe 1: Sausage and Egg Breakfast Bake

This savory casserole combines classic breakfast ingredients into a hearty dish that's perfect for any occasion. The combination of sausage, eggs, cheese, and bread creates a filling and satisfying meal.

Ingredients:

- 1 lb breakfast sausage
- 6 large eggs
- 2 cups milk
- 1 teaspoon mustard powder
- 1/2 teaspoon garlic powder
- 1/2 teaspoon onion powder
- Salt and pepper to taste
- 6 cups cubed bread (e.g., French bread or sourdough)
- 1 1/2 cups shredded cheddar cheese
- 1/4 cup chopped green onions (optional, for garnish)

Instructions:

1. Preheat oven to 350°F (175°C). Grease a 9x13-inch baking dish.

2. In a skillet over medium heat, cook the sausage until browned and crumbly. Drain excess fat and set aside.

3. In a large mixing bowl, whisk together eggs, milk, mustard powder, garlic powder, onion powder, salt, and pepper.

4. Layer the cubed bread in the prepared baking dish. Top with cooked sausage and 1 cup of shredded cheese.

5. Pour the egg mixture evenly over the bread and sausage. Press down lightly to ensure the bread absorbs the liquid.

6. Sprinkle the remaining cheese on top. Cover with aluminum foil and bake for 30 minutes.

7. Remove the foil and bake for an additional 15–20 minutes, or until the top is golden and the casserole is set.

8. Let cool for 5 minutes before garnishing with green onions and serving.

Tips:

- Use turkey or plant-based sausage for a lighter option.
- Add vegetables like sautéed mushrooms or bell peppers for extra flavor.

Recipe 2: French Toast Casserole

This sweet casserole transforms traditional French toast into a crowd-friendly dish with caramelized edges and a custardy center. It's perfect for brunch gatherings or holiday mornings.

Ingredients:
- 1 loaf of French bread or brioche, cut into 1-inch cubes
- 6 large eggs
- 2 cups milk
- 1 cup heavy cream
- 1/2 cup granulated sugar
- 1/2 cup brown sugar
- 1 teaspoon vanilla extract
- 1 teaspoon ground cinnamon
- 1/4 teaspoon nutmeg
- 1/4 cup unsalted butter, melted
- Powdered sugar and maple syrup (for serving)

Instructions:

1. Grease a 9x13-inch baking dish. Arrange the bread cubes evenly in the dish.

2. In a large bowl, whisk together eggs, milk, heavy cream, granulated sugar, brown sugar, vanilla, cinnamon, and nutmeg.

3. Pour the egg mixture over the bread cubes, pressing down gently to ensure the bread soaks up the custard.

4. Cover with plastic wrap and refrigerate for at least 4 hours or overnight.

5. Preheat oven to 350°F (175°C). Remove the casserole from the refrigerator and let it sit at room temperature for 20 minutes.

6. Drizzle the melted butter over the top. Bake for 45–50 minutes, or until the top is golden and the custard is set.

7. Let cool for 5 minutes before dusting with powdered sugar and serving with maple syrup.

Tips:
- Add sliced bananas or berries for a fruity twist.
- Substitute half the milk with eggnog for a festive holiday version.

Recipe 3: Vegetable Frittata Casserole

This savory, egg-based casserole is packed with fresh vegetables and cheese, making it a lighter option that's still hearty and flavorful.

Ingredients:

- 8 large eggs
- 1 cup milk
- 1/2 teaspoon salt
- 1/4 teaspoon black pepper
- 1/2 teaspoon dried basil
- 1 cup chopped spinach
- 1 cup diced zucchini
- 1/2 cup diced bell peppers
- 1/2 cup sliced mushrooms
- 1 cup shredded mozzarella cheese
- 1/4 cup grated Parmesan cheese

Instructions:

1. Preheat oven to 375°F (190°C). Grease an 8x8-inch baking dish.

2. In a large bowl, whisk together eggs, milk, salt, pepper, and basil.

3. Spread the spinach, zucchini, bell peppers, and mushrooms evenly in the baking dish.

4. Pour the egg mixture over the vegetables. Sprinkle with mozzarella and Parmesan cheese.

5. Bake for 30–35 minutes, or until the eggs are set and the top is golden.

6. Let cool for 5 minutes before slicing and serving.

Tips:

- Use leftover roasted vegetables for a quick and easy version.

- Add a sprinkle of red pepper flakes for a hint of heat.

Sweet and Savory Variations

1. Sweet Options

- Berry Delight: Add mixed berries and a streusel topping to French Toast Casserole.

- Cinnamon Roll Bake: Use cinnamon roll pieces instead of bread for a decadent treat.

2. Savory Options

- Southwestern Twist: Add chorizo, black beans, and pepper jack cheese to the Sausage and Egg Bake.

- Mediterranean Flavor: Incorporate feta, sun-dried tomatoes, and olives into the Vegetable Frittata.

Tips for Perfect Breakfast Casseroles

1. Plan Ahead

- Assemble casseroles the night before to save time in the morning.

- Use pre-cooked ingredients like roasted vegetables or cooked meats for faster preparation.

2. Use High-Quality Ingredients

- Opt for fresh eggs, whole milk, and artisanal bread for the best flavor and texture.

- Incorporate seasonal produce to highlight fresh flavors.

3. Layer Wisely

- Distribute ingredients evenly to ensure every bite is balanced.

- Press bread or other absorbent ingredients into liquid mixtures to prevent dry spots.

4. Adjust Cooking Times

- Check for doneness by inserting a knife into the center; it should come out clean when the casserole is fully cooked.

- Cover casseroles with foil if the top browns too quickly.

Conclusion

Breakfast and brunch casseroles are the ultimate solution for feeding a crowd or simplifying your mornings. With recipes like Sausage and Egg Breakfast Bake, French Toast Casserole, and Vegetable Frittata Casserole, you can cater to every palate and occasion. Sweet or savory, these versatile dishes are as comforting as they are practical. By planning ahead and customizing with your favorite ingredients, you can create memorable meals that bring people together and start the day on a delicious note.

Chapter 4: Vegetarian and Vegan Casseroles

Plant-based casseroles are not only a wholesome choice but also a testament to the versatility of vegetarian and vegan cooking. They are hearty, satisfying, and packed with nutrients, making them a hit at any dinner table, regardless of dietary preferences. Whether you're a seasoned vegan or simply looking to incorporate more meatless meals into your routine, vegetarian and vegan casseroles offer endless possibilities for creativity and flavor. This chapter introduces three standout recipes—Lentil Shepherd's Pie, Sweet Potato and Black Bean Enchilada Casserole, and Vegan Mac and Cheese Bake—and provides tips and substitutions to help you create flavorful, plant-based dishes that will please everyone.

The Appeal of Vegetarian and Vegan Casseroles

1. Health Benefits

- Nutrient-Rich: Packed with vegetables, legumes, and whole grains, plant-based casseroles are high in vitamins, fiber, and antioxidants.

- Heart-Healthy: Free of cholesterol and low in saturated fat, vegan casseroles support cardiovascular health.

2. Environmental Impact

Choosing plant-based meals reduces the carbon footprint associated with animal agriculture, making these dishes an eco-friendly choice.

3. Versatility

- Customizable: Easily adapt recipes to include seasonal produce or pantry staples.

- Dietary Flexibility: Accommodate gluten-free, soy-free, or nut-free diets with simple ingredient swaps.

4. Comfort and Satisfaction

Plant-based casseroles prove that meat isn't necessary for creating rich, hearty, and indulgent meals.

Recipe 1: Lentil Shepherd's Pie

This vegan twist on the classic British comfort food swaps the traditional meat filling for a flavorful lentil and vegetable base. Topped with creamy mashed potatoes, it's a dish that satisfies both vegans and omnivores alike.

Ingredients:

- 1 cup dried green or brown lentils
- 2 cups vegetable broth
- 1 tablespoon olive oil
- 1 medium onion, diced
- 2 carrots, diced
- 1 cup frozen peas
- 2 cloves garlic, minced
- 2 tablespoons tomato paste
- 1 tablespoon soy sauce or tamari
- 1 teaspoon dried thyme
- 1 teaspoon smoked paprika
- Salt and pepper to taste

For the Mashed Potato Topping:

- 4 large potatoes, peeled and chopped
- 1/4 cup plant-based milk
- 2 tablespoons vegan butter
- Salt and pepper to taste

Instructions:

1. Preheat oven to 375°F (190°C).

2. Cook lentils in vegetable broth according to package instructions. Drain and set aside.

3. In a large skillet, heat olive oil over medium heat. Sauté onion, carrots, and garlic until softened, about 5 minutes.

4. Add cooked lentils, tomato paste, soy sauce, thyme, smoked paprika, salt, and pepper. Stir well and cook for another 5 minutes. Stir in frozen peas.

5. Transfer the lentil mixture to a greased baking dish.

6. Boil potatoes in salted water until tender, about 15 minutes. Drain and mash with plant-based milk and vegan butter. Season with salt and pepper.

7. Spread the mashed potatoes evenly over the lentil mixture. Use a fork to create texture on the surface.

8. Bake for 20–25 minutes, or until the top is lightly golden. Let cool for 5 minutes before serving.

Tips:

- Substitute sweet potatoes for a slightly sweeter topping.
- Add mushrooms to the filling for extra depth of flavor.

Recipe 2: Sweet Potato and Black Bean Enchilada Casserole

This Southwestern-inspired casserole is a bold, zesty dish layered with sweet potatoes, black beans, and enchilada sauce. It's the perfect combination of sweet, smoky, and spicy.

Ingredients:

- 3 medium sweet potatoes, peeled and diced
- 1 tablespoon olive oil
- 1 teaspoon ground cumin
- 1 teaspoon smoked paprika
- Salt and pepper to taste
- 1 can (15 oz) black beans, drained and rinsed
- 1 can (15 oz) corn kernels, drained
- 2 cups enchilada sauce
- 8 small corn tortillas, cut into quarters
- 1 cup vegan shredded cheese (optional)
- Fresh cilantro and sliced jalapeños (for garnish)

Instructions:

1. Preheat oven to 375°F (190°C). Line a baking sheet with parchment paper.

2. Toss diced sweet potatoes with olive oil, cumin, smoked paprika, salt, and pepper. Spread on the baking sheet and roast for 20–25 minutes, or until tender.

3. In a large mixing bowl, combine roasted sweet potatoes, black beans, and corn.

4. Spread a thin layer of enchilada sauce in the bottom of a greased baking dish. Arrange a layer of tortilla pieces on top.

5. Add half of the sweet potato mixture and top with enchilada sauce. Repeat layers, finishing with enchilada sauce and vegan cheese if using.

6. Cover with aluminum foil and bake for 20 minutes. Remove foil and bake for an additional 10 minutes, or until bubbly.

7. Garnish with fresh cilantro and jalapeños before serving.

Tips:

- Swap sweet potatoes for butternut squash or pumpkin for a seasonal variation.

- Use homemade enchilada sauce for a fresher flavor.

Recipe 3: Vegan Mac and Cheese Bake

Creamy, cheesy, and entirely plant-based, this casserole is comfort food at its finest. A rich cashew-based sauce coats tender pasta, and a crispy breadcrumb topping adds the perfect finishing touch.

Ingredients:

- 1 lb elbow macaroni or other short pasta
- 1 cup raw cashews (soaked in hot water for 15 minutes)
- 1 1/2 cups unsweetened plant-based milk
- 1/4 cup nutritional yeast
- 2 tablespoons lemon juice
- 1 teaspoon garlic powder
- 1 teaspoon onion powder
- 1/2 teaspoon turmeric (for color)
- Salt and pepper to taste
- 1/2 cup panko breadcrumbs
- 2 tablespoons olive oil
- 1 teaspoon smoked paprika

Instructions:

1. Preheat oven to 375°F (190°C). Grease a 9x13-inch baking dish.

2. Cook pasta according to package instructions. Drain and set aside.

3. In a blender, combine soaked cashews, plant-based milk, nutritional yeast, lemon juice, garlic powder, onion powder, turmeric, salt, and pepper. Blend until smooth and creamy.

4. Toss cooked pasta with the sauce and transfer to the baking dish.

5. In a small bowl, mix panko breadcrumbs, olive oil, and smoked paprika. Sprinkle evenly over the casserole.

6. Bake for 20–25 minutes, or until the top is golden and crispy. Let cool for 5 minutes before serving.

Tips:

- Add sautéed spinach, broccoli, or peas for extra nutrition.

- Use gluten-free pasta and breadcrumbs for a gluten-free version.

Substitutions and Tips for Flavorful Vegan Casseroles

1. Dairy-Free Alternatives

- Cheese: Use nutritional yeast, cashew cream, or store-bought vegan cheese.

- Milk: Replace dairy milk with almond, soy, or oat milk.

2. Protein-Rich Additions

- Legumes: Incorporate lentils, chickpeas, or black beans for a hearty filling.

- Tofu or Tempeh: Crumble or dice for added protein and texture.

3. Flavor Enhancers

- Spices and Herbs: Use smoked paprika, cumin, turmeric, thyme, or rosemary for depth.

- Acidity: Add a splash of lemon juice or apple cider vinegar to brighten flavors.

4. Creative Toppings

- Use crushed tortilla chips, breadcrumbs, or roasted nuts to add crunch.

- Sprinkle fresh herbs or drizzle tahini for a fresh, vibrant finish.

Conclusion

Vegetarian and vegan casseroles prove that plant-based meals can be hearty, satisfying, and deeply flavorful. With recipes like Lentil Shepherd's Pie, Sweet Potato and Black Bean Enchilada Casserole, and Vegan Mac and Cheese Bake, you can create comforting, nutritious dishes that appeal to everyone. By exploring creative substitutions and flavor combinations, you'll discover that the possibilities for plant-based casseroles are truly endless. Let these recipes inspire you to experiment and enjoy the art of plant-based cooking.

Chapter 5: Global-Inspired Casseroles

Casseroles transcend cultural boundaries, serving as a canvas for flavors from around the world. Every culture has its own version of a one-dish meal that brings people together, whether it's a creamy Greek Moussaka, a hearty Mexican Tamale Pie, or a comforting Italian Eggplant Parmesan Bake. Global-inspired casseroles are not only delicious but also a delightful way to explore international cuisines from the comfort of your kitchen. This chapter delves into three standout recipes, pairing ideas for complete meals, and tips for incorporating authentic flavors into your casseroles.

The Universal Appeal of Casseroles

1. A Culinary Bridge Across Cultures

Casseroles are a universal food concept, blending ingredients into a single dish and baking them to perfection. While techniques and ingredients vary, the essence remains the same:

- Greek Moussaka: A layered casserole that combines eggplant, meat sauce, and béchamel for a Mediterranean feast.

- Mexican Tamale Pie: A vibrant casserole featuring spiced meat, beans, and cornbread crust.

- Italian Eggplant Parmesan Bake: A classic Italian dish showcasing eggplant, marinara, and gooey cheese.

2. Why Global-Inspired Casseroles Work

- Adaptability: Ingredients can often be substituted to suit local availability.

- Convenience: These dishes are easy to prepare and can feed a crowd.

- Flavor Exploration: Global casseroles introduce diverse spices, herbs, and textures to your table.

Recipe 1: Greek Moussaka

Moussaka is a quintessential Greek dish that layers roasted eggplant, spiced meat sauce, and creamy béchamel for a casserole that's rich, hearty, and full of Mediterranean flavors.

Ingredients:

For the Eggplant:

- 2 large eggplants, sliced into 1/4-inch rounds
- 2 tablespoons olive oil
- Salt and pepper to taste

For the Meat Sauce:

- 1 tablespoon olive oil
- 1 medium onion, diced
- 2 garlic cloves, minced
- 1 lb ground lamb or beef
- 1 can (14 oz) diced tomatoes
- 2 tablespoons tomato paste
- 1 teaspoon ground cinnamon
- 1 teaspoon dried oregano
- Salt and pepper to taste

For the Béchamel Sauce:

- 4 tablespoons butter
- 4 tablespoons all-purpose flour
- 2 cups milk
- 1/4 cup grated Parmesan cheese
- A pinch of nutmeg
- Salt and pepper to taste

Instructions:

1. Preheat oven to 375°F (190°C). Grease a 9x13-inch baking dish.

2. Lay eggplant slices on a baking sheet. Brush with olive oil, season with salt and pepper, and roast for 20 minutes, flipping halfway.

3. While the eggplant is roasting, heat olive oil in a skillet over medium heat. Sauté onion and garlic until softened. Add ground lamb and cook until browned.

4. Stir in diced tomatoes, tomato paste, cinnamon, oregano, salt, and pepper. Simmer for 10 minutes.

5. To make the béchamel sauce, melt butter in a saucepan over medium heat. Whisk in flour and cook for 2 minutes. Gradually add milk, whisking constantly until thickened. Stir in Parmesan, nutmeg, salt, and pepper.

6. Layer half of the eggplant slices in the baking dish. Spread the meat sauce over the eggplant, followed by the remaining eggplant slices. Pour the béchamel sauce evenly over the top.

7. Bake for 30–35 minutes, or until golden and bubbly. Let cool for 10 minutes before serving.

Tips:

- Use ground turkey for a leaner version.

- Add a layer of sliced potatoes for extra heartiness.

Recipe 2: Mexican Tamale Pie

Tamale Pie is a flavorful casserole inspired by the traditional Mexican tamale. This version layers spiced meat, beans, and vegetables under a golden cornbread crust.

Ingredients:

For the Filling:

- 1 lb ground beef or turkey

- 1 medium onion, diced

- 2 garlic cloves, minced

- 1 can (14 oz) diced tomatoes

- 1 can (15 oz) black beans, drained and rinsed

- 1 cup corn kernels (fresh, frozen, or canned)

- 1 tablespoon chili powder

- 1 teaspoon cumin

- 1 teaspoon smoked paprika

- Salt and pepper to taste

For the Cornbread Topping:

- 1 cup cornmeal

- 1 cup all-purpose flour

- 1 tablespoon sugar
- 1 teaspoon baking powder
- 1/2 teaspoon baking soda
- 1/2 teaspoon salt
- 1 cup buttermilk (or plant-based milk with 1 tablespoon vinegar)
- 1 large egg
- 2 tablespoons melted butter

Instructions:

1. Preheat oven to 375°F (190°C). Grease a 9x13-inch baking dish.

2. In a skillet, cook ground beef over medium heat until browned. Drain excess fat and add onion and garlic. Cook until softened.

3. Stir in diced tomatoes, black beans, corn, chili powder, cumin, smoked paprika, salt, and pepper. Simmer for 5–7 minutes.

4. Spread the meat mixture evenly in the baking dish.

5. In a mixing bowl, combine cornmeal, flour, sugar, baking powder, baking soda, and salt. Add buttermilk, egg, and melted butter. Stir until just combined.

6. Spread the cornbread batter over the filling. Bake for 25–30 minutes, or until the cornbread is golden and a toothpick inserted into the center comes out clean.

7. Let cool for 5 minutes before serving.

Tips:

- Add diced jalapeños or shredded cheese to the cornbread batter for extra flavor.

- Serve with salsa, sour cream, or guacamole.

Recipe 3: Italian Eggplant Parmesan Bake

This Italian classic layers tender eggplant slices with marinara sauce and gooey cheese for a comforting and satisfying vegetarian dish.

Ingredients:

- 2 large eggplants, sliced into 1/4-inch rounds
- 1 cup all-purpose flour
- 2 large eggs, beaten
- 1 1/2 cups breadcrumbs
- 1 cup grated Parmesan cheese

- 2 cups marinara sauce
- 2 cups shredded mozzarella cheese
- Fresh basil leaves (for garnish)

Instructions:

1. Preheat oven to 375°F (190°C). Line a baking sheet with parchment paper.

2. Dredge each eggplant slice in flour, dip in beaten eggs, and coat with breadcrumbs. Arrange on the baking sheet and bake for 20 minutes, flipping halfway.

3. Spread a thin layer of marinara sauce in a greased baking dish. Layer eggplant slices over the sauce, followed by more marinara, mozzarella, and Parmesan. Repeat layers, finishing with cheese on top.

4. Bake for 25–30 minutes, or until bubbly and golden. Garnish with fresh basil before serving.

Tips:

- Use gluten-free breadcrumbs for a gluten-free version.
- Add a layer of sautéed spinach for extra nutrition.

Pairing Casseroles with Sides for a Complete Meal

1. Greek Moussaka
    - Side: Greek salad with cucumbers, tomatoes, olives, and feta.
    - Drink: A dry red wine like Merlot or a refreshing glass of white Retsina.
2. Mexican Tamale Pie
    - Side: Fresh guacamole and tortilla chips or a crisp cabbage slaw.
    - Drink: A zesty margarita or a light Mexican lager.
3. Italian Eggplant Parmesan Bake
    - Side: Garlic bread and a simple arugula salad with lemon vinaigrette.
    - Drink: A glass of Chianti or a sparkling San Pellegrino.

Tips for Adding Authentic Flavors

1. Spices and Herbs: Use fresh or dried herbs and spices that are staples in the cuisine, like oregano for Greek dishes or cumin for Mexican recipes.

2. Cheese Substitutes: For vegan adaptations, use plant-based cheese that melts well and aligns with the dish's flavors.

3. Local Ingredients: Incorporate fresh, seasonal, or locally sourced ingredients to elevate the dish's quality.

Conclusion

Global-inspired casseroles like Greek Moussaka, Mexican Tamale Pie, and Italian Eggplant Parmesan Bake showcase the diversity and creativity of international cuisines. These dishes not only introduce bold flavors and textures but also bring people together in a celebration of cultural richness. By pairing them with complementary sides and drinks, you can create complete meals that transport your taste buds across the globe. Let these recipes inspire you to explore, experiment, and savor the world of casseroles.

Chapter 6: Casseroles for Two

Casseroles are often associated with large gatherings, potlucks, and family dinners, but they can also be adapted for smaller households or intimate meals. A well-prepared casserole for two is the perfect solution for cozy dinners, allowing you to enjoy all the comfort and flavor of a classic casserole without the hassle of leftovers. In this chapter, we explore how to scale down recipes effectively, featuring delicious and satisfying dishes like Mini Chicken Pot Pies, Creamy Broccoli and Rice Casserole, and Individual Ziti Bakes. We also cover tips on portion control and creative storage solutions to ensure nothing goes to waste.

Why Make Casseroles for Two?

1. Ideal for Smaller Households
   - Perfect for couples, roommates, or individuals who want to cook just enough for one meal and perhaps a light lunch the next day.
   2. Reduces Food Waste
   - Scaling down ensures you prepare only what you need, minimizing leftovers and waste.
   3. Customizable
   - Smaller portions make it easier to experiment with flavors and cater to individual preferences.
   4. Saves Time
   - Smaller casseroles often cook faster and require less preparation, making them ideal for weeknight dinners.

How to Scale Down Recipes

1. Adjust Ingredient Quantities
   - Divide ingredients in half or by a third, depending on the original recipe's size.
   - Use online calculators to help scale measurements accurately.
   2. Use Smaller Dishes

- Opt for smaller baking dishes, such as 8x8-inch pans, ramekins, or individual casserole dishes.

3. Modify Cooking Times

- Smaller casseroles often require shorter baking times. Check for doneness earlier to avoid overcooking.

4. Balance Flavors

- Be cautious when scaling down seasonings; start with less and adjust to taste.

Recipe 1: Mini Chicken Pot Pies

These individual pot pies are a comforting classic scaled down for two. With a flaky crust and creamy chicken filling, they're perfect for a cozy dinner.

Ingredients:

- 1 tablespoon butter
- 1 small onion, diced
- 1 small carrot, diced
- 1 stalk celery, diced
- 1 cup cooked chicken, shredded
- 1/2 cup frozen peas
- 1/2 cup chicken broth
- 1/4 cup heavy cream
- 1 tablespoon all-purpose flour
- 1/4 teaspoon dried thyme
- Salt and pepper to taste
- 1 sheet puff pastry, thawed
- 1 egg, beaten (for egg wash)

Instructions:

1. Preheat oven to 400°F (200°C). Grease two 8-ounce ramekins or small baking dishes.

2. In a skillet, melt butter over medium heat. Sauté onion, carrot, and celery until softened, about 5 minutes.

3. Stir in flour and cook for 1 minute. Gradually add chicken broth, stirring until thickened. Add heavy cream, thyme, salt, and pepper.

4. Mix in cooked chicken and peas. Divide the mixture evenly between the prepared ramekins.

5. Cut the puff pastry into two circles slightly larger than the ramekins. Place a pastry circle over each ramekin, pressing the edges to seal. Cut small slits in the top to allow steam to escape. Brush with beaten egg.

6. Bake for 20–25 minutes, or until the pastry is golden and puffed. Let cool for 5 minutes before serving.

Tips:

- Use leftover rotisserie chicken for a quick shortcut.

- Add diced potatoes or mushrooms for extra heartiness.

Recipe 2: Creamy Broccoli and Rice Casserole

This vegetarian casserole is creamy, cheesy, and packed with broccoli. It's a simple yet satisfying dish that's perfect for two.

Ingredients:

- 1 tablespoon butter
- 1 small onion, finely chopped
- 1 clove garlic, minced
- 1 cup cooked rice (white or brown)
- 1 cup broccoli florets, steamed
- 1/2 cup shredded cheddar cheese
- 1/4 cup grated Parmesan cheese
- 1/2 cup milk
- 1 tablespoon all-purpose flour
- 1/4 teaspoon mustard powder
- Salt and pepper to taste
- 1/4 cup breadcrumbs (optional, for topping)

Instructions:

1. Preheat oven to 375°F (190°C). Grease a small baking dish or two 8-ounce ramekins.

2. In a skillet, melt butter over medium heat. Sauté onion and garlic until softened. Stir in flour and cook for 1 minute.

3. Gradually whisk in milk and mustard powder, cooking until thickened. Remove from heat and stir in cheddar and Parmesan cheese until melted. Season with salt and pepper.

4. Combine the cheese sauce, cooked rice, and steamed broccoli. Transfer to the prepared dish(es).

5. If desired, sprinkle breadcrumbs on top for added crunch. Bake for 20–25 minutes, or until bubbly and golden.

Tips:

- Swap the rice for quinoa or cauliflower rice for a lower-carb option.

- Add sautéed mushrooms or diced bell peppers for extra vegetables.

Recipe 3: Individual Ziti Bakes

These cheesy, saucy pasta bakes are a delightful take on classic baked ziti, perfect for two.

Ingredients:

- 1 cup cooked ziti or penne pasta
- 1 cup marinara sauce
- 1/4 cup ricotta cheese
- 1/2 cup shredded mozzarella cheese
- 1/4 cup grated Parmesan cheese
- 1/2 teaspoon dried basil
- 1/2 teaspoon dried oregano
- Salt and pepper to taste

Instructions:

1. Preheat oven to 375°F (190°C). Grease two 8-ounce ramekins or small baking dishes.

2. In a mixing bowl, combine cooked pasta, marinara sauce, ricotta cheese, basil, oregano, salt, and pepper.

3. Divide the pasta mixture evenly between the ramekins. Top each with mozzarella and Parmesan cheese.

4. Bake for 20 minutes, or until the cheese is bubbly and golden. Let cool for 5 minutes before serving.

Tips:

- Add cooked Italian sausage or sautéed vegetables for variety.

- Use store-bought marinara for convenience, or make your own for a fresher taste.

Portion Control and Storage Tips

1. Portion Control

- Individual Dishes: Use ramekins or mini casserole dishes for perfectly portioned servings.

- Measuring Tools: Weigh or measure ingredients to ensure balanced portions.

2. Storage Solutions

- Refrigeration: Store leftovers in airtight containers for up to 3 days. Reheat in the oven or microwave.

- Freezing: Wrap uncooked casseroles tightly in foil and freeze for up to 3 months. Thaw overnight in the refrigerator before baking.

3. Avoiding Waste

- Repurpose leftovers:

- Pot Pie Filling: Use as a topping for toast or biscuits.

- Broccoli and Rice Mixture: Stir into an omelet or stuff into bell peppers.

- Ziti Bake: Toss with additional pasta or use as a pizza topping.

Conclusion

Casseroles for two offer the perfect balance of flavor, convenience, and portion control, making them ideal for smaller households or intimate meals. Recipes like Mini Chicken Pot Pies, Creamy Broccoli and Rice Casserole, and Individual Ziti Bakes provide all the comfort of classic casseroles without the excess. With smart scaling techniques and thoughtful storage solutions, you can enjoy the satisfaction of home-cooked casseroles tailored to your needs, any night of the week. Let these recipes inspire you to embrace the joy of cooking for two.

Chapter 7: Healthy and Light Casseroles

Casseroles are often associated with indulgence, but they can also be nourishing, light, and packed with wholesome ingredients. Healthy casseroles combine the comforting appeal of traditional recipes with a focus on balanced nutrition, making them a perfect choice for those looking to enjoy satisfying meals without sacrificing health goals. In this chapter, we'll explore how to balance flavor and nutrition in casseroles, with recipes for Quinoa and Kale Casserole, Low-Carb Zucchini Lasagna, and Mediterranean Chicken and Veggie Bake. Additionally, we'll provide tips for reducing calories, boosting nutrients, and creating casseroles that are as healthy as they are delicious.

Balancing Flavor and Nutrition in Casseroles

1. The Role of Ingredients

- Whole Grains: Incorporating grains like quinoa, farro, or brown rice provides fiber and essential nutrients.

- Vegetables: Adding a variety of vegetables increases vitamins, minerals, and antioxidants while enhancing flavor and texture.

- Lean Proteins: Opt for chicken, turkey, fish, or plant-based proteins like tofu and legumes for a healthier protein source.

- Healthy Fats: Use olive oil, avocado, or nuts to add richness without relying on saturated fats.

2. Flavor Boosters

- Herbs and Spices: Fresh herbs like basil, parsley, and cilantro, or spices like cumin, paprika, and turmeric, elevate flavor without adding calories.

- Citrus and Vinegars: A splash of lemon juice or balsamic vinegar brightens dishes and balances richness.

- Natural Sweeteners: Small amounts of honey, maple syrup, or fruit can add depth and counterbalance savory flavors.

3. Cooking Techniques

- Roasting: Enhances the natural sweetness of vegetables.

- Layering: Strategically layering ingredients ensures even cooking and optimal flavor distribution.

- Blending: Use pureed vegetables like cauliflower or butternut squash to create creamy sauces without heavy cream.

Recipe 1: Quinoa and Kale Casserole

This vibrant casserole combines nutrient-packed quinoa and kale with creamy cheese and crunchy breadcrumbs for a dish that's both healthy and indulgent.

Ingredients:

- 1 cup quinoa, rinsed
- 2 cups vegetable broth
- 1 tablespoon olive oil
- 1 small onion, diced
- 2 garlic cloves, minced
- 4 cups kale, chopped
- 1/2 cup shredded mozzarella cheese
- 1/4 cup grated Parmesan cheese
- 1/4 cup breadcrumbs (optional)
- 1/4 teaspoon crushed red pepper flakes (optional)
- Salt and pepper to taste

Instructions:

1. Preheat oven to 375°F (190°C). Grease an 8x8-inch baking dish.

2. Cook quinoa in vegetable broth according to package instructions. Fluff with a fork and set aside.

3. In a skillet, heat olive oil over medium heat. Sauté onion and garlic until softened, about 3 minutes. Add kale and cook until wilted, about 5 minutes. Season with salt, pepper, and red pepper flakes if using.

4. Combine cooked quinoa, kale mixture, mozzarella, and Parmesan in a large bowl. Mix until evenly combined.

5. Transfer the mixture to the prepared baking dish. Sprinkle breadcrumbs over the top if desired.

6. Bake for 20–25 minutes, or until the top is golden and the casserole is heated through.

Tips:

- Swap kale for spinach or Swiss chard for a different flavor profile.

- Add roasted sweet potatoes or butternut squash for extra sweetness and texture.

Recipe 2: Low-Carb Zucchini Lasagna

This low-carb lasagna uses thinly sliced zucchini instead of pasta, creating a lighter version of the Italian classic without sacrificing flavor.

Ingredients:

- 3 medium zucchinis, thinly sliced lengthwise
- 1 tablespoon olive oil
- 1 lb ground turkey or chicken
- 1 small onion, diced
- 2 garlic cloves, minced
- 1 can (14 oz) crushed tomatoes
- 1 teaspoon dried basil
- 1 teaspoon dried oregano
- 1 cup ricotta cheese
- 1/2 cup shredded mozzarella cheese
- 1/4 cup grated Parmesan cheese
- Salt and pepper to taste

Instructions:

1. Preheat oven to 375°F (190°C). Grease a 9x9-inch baking dish.

2. Lay zucchini slices on paper towels. Sprinkle with salt and let sit for 10 minutes to draw out moisture. Pat dry.

3. In a skillet, heat olive oil over medium heat. Cook ground turkey, onion, and garlic until the meat is browned and the onion is softened. Stir in crushed tomatoes, basil, oregano, salt, and pepper. Simmer for 10 minutes.

4. In a mixing bowl, combine ricotta cheese, half of the mozzarella, and half of the Parmesan.

5. Spread a thin layer of the meat sauce in the baking dish. Layer zucchini slices over the sauce, followed by a layer of the ricotta mixture. Repeat layers, finishing with the remaining mozzarella and Parmesan on top.

6. Cover with foil and bake for 20 minutes. Remove foil and bake for an additional 15 minutes, or until the cheese is golden and bubbly. Let rest for 10 minutes before serving.

Tips:

- Use a mandoline slicer for even zucchini slices.

- Add mushrooms, spinach, or bell peppers to the meat sauce for extra vegetables.

Recipe 3: Mediterranean Chicken and Veggie Bake

This colorful casserole features tender chicken, vibrant vegetables, and Mediterranean flavors like olives, lemon, and oregano.

Ingredients:

- 2 boneless, skinless chicken breasts, cut into bite-sized pieces
- 1 small red onion, sliced
- 1 red bell pepper, sliced
- 1 yellow bell pepper, sliced
- 1 cup cherry tomatoes
- 1/2 cup pitted Kalamata olives
- 2 tablespoons olive oil
- 1 teaspoon dried oregano
- 1 teaspoon garlic powder
- Juice of 1 lemon
- Salt and pepper to taste
- 1/4 cup crumbled feta cheese (optional)

Instructions:

1. Preheat oven to 400°F (200°C). Grease a 9x13-inch baking dish.

2. In a large bowl, combine chicken, onion, bell peppers, cherry tomatoes, olives, olive oil, oregano, garlic powder, lemon juice, salt, and pepper. Toss to coat evenly.

3. Transfer the mixture to the baking dish, spreading it out in an even layer.

4. Bake for 25–30 minutes, or until the chicken is cooked through and the vegetables are tender.

5. Sprinkle with feta cheese before serving, if desired.

Tips:

- Serve over a bed of quinoa or whole-grain couscous for a complete meal.

- Add zucchini or eggplant for more Mediterranean-inspired flavors.

Tips for Reducing Calories and Increasing Nutrients

1. Use Whole Grains

Replace refined grains like white rice or pasta with quinoa, farro, or brown rice for added fiber and nutrients.

2. Incorporate More Vegetables

- Use vegetables as substitutes for higher-calorie ingredients, like zucchini in place of lasagna noodles.

- Add roasted or steamed vegetables to casseroles for additional volume and flavor.

3. Choose Lean Proteins

Opt for chicken breast, turkey, fish, or plant-based proteins like beans, lentils, or tofu to reduce saturated fat content.

4. Lighten Creamy Sauces

- Replace heavy cream with low-fat milk, Greek yogurt, or pureed cauliflower.

- Use smaller amounts of cheese, opting for stronger-flavored varieties like Parmesan or feta for maximum impact.

5. Minimize Added Fats

- Use nonstick cooking sprays instead of butter to grease pans.

- Drizzle olive oil lightly instead of using larger quantities.

6. Control Portions

Serve casseroles with a side salad or soup to keep portion sizes reasonable while still feeling full and satisfied.

Conclusion

Healthy and light casseroles like Quinoa and Kale Casserole, Low-Carb Zucchini Lasagna, and Mediterranean Chicken and Veggie Bake prove that nutritious meals can be just as satisfying as their indulgent counterparts. By incorporating whole grains, vegetables, lean proteins, and healthier cooking techniques, you can create casseroles that are both flavorful and nourishing. With a little creativity and these recipes as a starting point, you'll be able to enjoy comforting, wholesome meals that fit seamlessly into a balanced lifestyle.

Chapter 8: Family-Friendly Casseroles

Family-friendly casseroles are a lifesaver for busy households, offering a versatile, convenient, and delicious solution to dinnertime dilemmas. These one-dish meals cater to all ages and are especially loved by kids for their comforting flavors and familiar ingredients. Whether it's the cheesy goodness of Pizza Casserole, the crispy delight of Tater Tot Casserole, or the creamy satisfaction of Cheesy Chicken and Broccoli Bake, these dishes are guaranteed to bring everyone to the table. In this chapter, we'll share recipes that the whole family will love, along with tips on customizing casseroles to please even the pickiest eaters.

Why Casseroles Are Perfect for Families

1. Convenient and Time-Saving

   - One-Dish Meals: Fewer dishes mean less cleanup, making casseroles ideal for busy weeknights.

   - Prep Ahead: Many casseroles can be assembled in advance and baked when needed, saving time during hectic evenings.

   2. Adaptable for All Ages

   - Kid-Approved Ingredients: Incorporating familiar flavors like cheese, pasta, and mild seasonings makes casseroles appealing to children.

   - Customizable: Easy to adjust ingredients to suit dietary needs and preferences.

   3. Budget-Friendly

   - Stretching Ingredients: Combining proteins, vegetables, and grains into a single dish maximizes the use of pantry staples and leftovers.

Recipe 1: Pizza Casserole

Pizza Casserole takes the flavors of a classic pizza and transforms them into a fun, family-friendly dish. With layers of pasta, marinara, cheese, and your favorite toppings, it's an instant hit with kids and adults alike.

   Ingredients:

   - 8 oz rotini or penne pasta

- 2 cups marinara sauce
- 1 cup shredded mozzarella cheese
- 1/2 cup grated Parmesan cheese
- 1/2 cup mini pepperoni slices
- 1/2 cup cooked Italian sausage (optional)
- 1/4 cup sliced black olives (optional)
- 1/4 teaspoon garlic powder
- 1/4 teaspoon dried oregano

Instructions:

1. Preheat oven to 375°F (190°C). Grease a 9x13-inch baking dish.

2. Cook pasta according to package instructions until al dente. Drain and set aside.

3. In a large mixing bowl, combine cooked pasta, marinara sauce, garlic powder, and oregano. Mix well.

4. Spread half of the pasta mixture into the prepared baking dish. Top with half of the mozzarella and Parmesan cheese. Add a layer of mini pepperoni, sausage, and olives if using.

5. Repeat layers with the remaining pasta mixture, cheese, and toppings.

6. Bake for 20–25 minutes, or until the cheese is melted and bubbly. Let cool for 5 minutes before serving.

Tips:

- Swap pepperoni for diced ham or cooked chicken for a milder flavor.

- Add diced bell peppers, mushrooms, or spinach to sneak in extra veggies.

Recipe 2: Tater Tot Casserole

This crispy, cheesy casserole is a kid-favorite that combines ground beef, vegetables, and golden tater tots for a fun and satisfying meal.

Ingredients:

- 1 lb ground beef or turkey
- 1 small onion, diced
- 1 can (10.5 oz) cream of mushroom soup (or homemade)
- 1 cup frozen mixed vegetables (peas, carrots, and corn)
- 1 cup shredded cheddar cheese
- 1 bag (16 oz) frozen tater tots

- Salt and pepper to taste

Instructions:

1. Preheat oven to 375°F (190°C). Grease a 9x13-inch baking dish.

2. In a skillet, cook ground beef and onion over medium heat until browned. Drain excess fat and season with salt and pepper.

3. Stir in cream of mushroom soup and frozen vegetables. Mix until combined.

4. Spread the beef mixture evenly in the prepared baking dish. Sprinkle shredded cheddar cheese on top.

5. Arrange tater tots in a single layer over the cheese.

6. Bake for 30–35 minutes, or until the tater tots are golden and crispy. Let cool for 5 minutes before serving.

Tips:

- Use ground chicken or plant-based meat for a healthier or vegetarian option.

- Swap cream of mushroom soup for cream of chicken or a dairy-free alternative.

Recipe 3: Cheesy Chicken and Broccoli Bake

This creamy casserole combines tender chicken, broccoli, and rice in a cheesy sauce for a comforting dish that's both nutritious and delicious.

Ingredients:

- 2 cups cooked chicken, shredded

- 1 1/2 cups cooked rice (white or brown)

- 2 cups broccoli florets, steamed

- 1 can (10.5 oz) cream of chicken soup (or homemade)

- 1/2 cup milk

- 1 cup shredded cheddar cheese

- 1/4 cup grated Parmesan cheese

- Salt and pepper to taste

Instructions:

1. Preheat oven to 375°F (190°C). Grease a 9x13-inch baking dish.

2. In a large mixing bowl, combine cream of chicken soup, milk, salt, and pepper. Stir in shredded chicken, cooked rice, and steamed broccoli.

3. Transfer the mixture to the prepared baking dish. Sprinkle cheddar and Parmesan cheese evenly over the top.

4. Bake for 20–25 minutes, or until the cheese is melted and bubbly. Let cool for 5 minutes before serving.

Tips:

- Substitute cauliflower rice for a lower-carb option.

- Add sautéed mushrooms or diced bell peppers for extra flavor.

Customizing Casseroles for Picky Eaters

1. Make It Interactive

- Let kids help assemble casseroles by layering ingredients or adding toppings like cheese or breadcrumbs.

- Offer a variety of toppings so everyone can customize their portion.

2. Hide the Veggies

- Blend vegetables like spinach or carrots into sauces to boost nutrition without detection.

- Grate or finely chop veggies to mix into the casserole base.

3. Stick to Familiar Flavors

- Use ingredients that kids already enjoy, like pasta, cheese, or mild proteins.

- Gradually introduce new flavors or vegetables alongside their favorites.

4. Create Mini Casseroles

- Prepare individual portions in ramekins for personalized servings.

- Smaller casseroles can also make it easier to introduce variations.

Portion Control and Leftovers

1. Portion Sizes

- For younger children, serve smaller portions and allow seconds if they're still hungry.

- Pair casseroles with simple sides like a salad or fruit to create a balanced meal.

2. Storing Leftovers

- Refrigerate casseroles in airtight containers for up to 3 days.

- Freeze portions for up to 3 months, reheating in the oven or microwave as needed.

3. Repurposing Leftovers

- Transform leftover casserole into wraps, sandwiches, or stuffed bell peppers.

- Use as a topping for baked potatoes or mix into soups for a new meal.

Tips for Making Family-Friendly Casseroles

1. Keep It Simple: Use straightforward recipes with familiar ingredients to ensure wide appeal.

2. Plan Ahead: Double recipes and freeze half for future meals.

3. Balance Flavors: Avoid overly spicy or strong flavors for younger palates, but keep seasoning well-rounded.

4. Add a Crunchy Topping: Use breadcrumbs, crushed crackers, or crispy onions to add texture and visual appeal.

Conclusion

Family-friendly casseroles like Pizza Casserole, Tater Tot Casserole, and Cheesy Chicken and Broccoli Bake are perfect for bringing everyone to the table. These recipes are easy to prepare, customizable, and packed with comforting flavors that kids and adults alike will enjoy. By tailoring casseroles to suit picky eaters and repurposing leftovers creatively, you can make mealtime stress-free and enjoyable for the whole family. Let these recipes inspire your next family dinner and prove that casseroles truly are the ultimate crowd-pleaser.

Chapter 9: Holiday and Festive Casseroles

The holidays are a time for gathering with loved ones, sharing meals, and celebrating traditions. Amidst the hustle and bustle, casseroles are a practical and comforting choice for creating memorable, show-stopping dishes. Whether it's a classic Green Bean Casserole, a creamy Sweet Potato Casserole, or the hearty indulgence of Baked Ham and Scalloped Potatoes, these recipes are perfect for festive occasions. This chapter explores how to create holiday-worthy casseroles, complete with make-ahead tips to ensure stress-free celebrations.

Why Casseroles Are Perfect for the Holidays

1. Versatility

Casseroles fit seamlessly into any holiday menu, whether as a side dish, main course, or dessert. Their adaptability makes them suitable for:
- Classic Traditions: Recipes like Green Bean Casserole offer a nostalgic connection to family gatherings.
- Modern Twists: Creative ingredients and flavors can breathe new life into holiday favorites.
- Diverse Diets: Easily adjusted for gluten-free, vegetarian, or vegan preferences.

2. Stress-Free Preparation

- Make-Ahead Options: Many casseroles can be prepared in advance and simply baked before serving.
- One-Dish Meals: They minimize dishwashing and maximize convenience in busy kitchens.

3. Crowd-Pleasing Appeal

- Casseroles are hearty, satisfying, and designed to feed a group, making them perfect for holiday celebrations.

Recipe 1: Classic Green Bean Casserole

This timeless side dish has been a staple at holiday tables for generations. Its creamy sauce, tender green beans, and crispy onion topping make it a crowd favorite.

Ingredients:
- 1 lb fresh green beans, trimmed (or 2 cans, drained)
- 1 can (10.5 oz) cream of mushroom soup
- 1/2 cup milk
- 1/4 teaspoon garlic powder
- 1/4 teaspoon black pepper
- 1 cup French-fried onions

Instructions:
1. Preheat oven to 350°F (175°C). Grease a 9x13-inch baking dish.
2. If using fresh green beans, blanch them in boiling water for 3–4 minutes, then drain and set aside.
3. In a mixing bowl, combine cream of mushroom soup, milk, garlic powder, and black pepper. Stir until smooth.
4. Add green beans to the soup mixture and mix until evenly coated.
5. Transfer the mixture to the prepared baking dish. Spread evenly and top with French-fried onions.
6. Bake for 25–30 minutes, or until bubbly and golden. Serve hot.

Tips:
- Use a homemade mushroom sauce for a fresher, less processed option.
- Add sliced mushrooms or water chestnuts for extra texture.

Recipe 2: Sweet Potato Casserole

Sweet Potato Casserole is a sweet, creamy, and indulgent holiday classic. The marshmallow or pecan topping adds a festive touch that's sure to delight guests of all ages.

Ingredients:

- 4 large sweet potatoes, peeled and cubed
- 1/4 cup unsalted butter, melted
- 1/4 cup brown sugar
- 1/4 cup maple syrup
- 1/2 teaspoon cinnamon
- 1/4 teaspoon nutmeg
- 1/4 teaspoon salt
- 1 cup mini marshmallows (optional)
- 1/2 cup chopped pecans (optional)

Instructions:

1. Preheat oven to 375°F (190°C). Grease a 9x9-inch baking dish.

2. Boil sweet potatoes in salted water until tender, about 15 minutes. Drain and mash until smooth.

3. In a large bowl, combine mashed sweet potatoes, melted butter, brown sugar, maple syrup, cinnamon, nutmeg, and salt. Mix well.

4. Transfer the mixture to the prepared baking dish and spread evenly.

5. Top with marshmallows and/or pecans, depending on preference.

6. Bake for 20–25 minutes, or until the topping is golden and bubbly. Serve warm.

Tips:

- For a vegan version, use plant-based butter and marshmallows.
- Add a splash of orange juice for a citrusy twist.

Recipe 3: Baked Ham and Scalloped Potatoes

This casserole combines tender ham slices with layers of creamy, cheesy scalloped potatoes for a decadent holiday centerpiece.

Ingredients:

- 1 1/2 lbs Yukon Gold potatoes, thinly sliced
- 1 cup cooked ham, diced
- 2 tablespoons unsalted butter
- 2 tablespoons all-purpose flour
- 1 1/2 cups milk
- 1 cup shredded cheddar cheese
- 1/2 teaspoon garlic powder

- Salt and pepper to taste
- 1/4 cup grated Parmesan cheese (optional)
Instructions:

1. Preheat oven to 375°F (190°C). Grease a 9x13-inch baking dish.

2. In a saucepan, melt butter over medium heat. Whisk in flour and cook for 1 minute. Gradually add milk, whisking constantly, until thickened. Remove from heat and stir in cheddar cheese, garlic powder, salt, and pepper.

3. Layer half of the potato slices in the baking dish. Top with half of the diced ham and half of the cheese sauce. Repeat layers with the remaining potatoes, ham, and sauce.

4. Sprinkle Parmesan cheese over the top, if using. Cover with aluminum foil and bake for 40 minutes.

5. Remove foil and bake for an additional 20 minutes, or until the potatoes are tender and the top is golden. Let cool for 10 minutes before serving.

Tips:
- Add caramelized onions or sautéed mushrooms for extra flavor.
- Substitute sweet potatoes for a unique twist.

Make-Ahead Tips for Stress-Free Holiday Meals

1. Plan Ahead
   - Select casseroles that complement your holiday menu and dietary needs.
   - Prepare a shopping list to ensure all ingredients are on hand.
2. Assemble Early
   - Most casseroles can be assembled a day or two in advance and refrigerated until ready to bake.
   - Cover tightly with plastic wrap or foil to maintain freshness.
3. Optimize Freezing
   - Freeze casseroles like Green Bean or Sweet Potato Casserole without their toppings. Add toppings just before baking to preserve texture.
   - Use freezer-safe containers and label them with the dish name and baking instructions.
4. Efficient Baking
   - Bake multiple casseroles simultaneously by adjusting oven racks and rotating dishes halfway through cooking.

- Use a slow cooker for casseroles that don't require a crispy topping.
5. Reheating Leftovers
- Reheat casseroles in the oven at 350°F (175°C) for 20–30 minutes, or until warmed through. Cover with foil to prevent drying out.

Presentation and Pairing Ideas

1. Green Bean Casserole
   - Pair With: Roasted turkey, glazed ham, or stuffing.
   - Presentation: Garnish with crispy shallots or fresh parsley for an elegant touch.
   2. Sweet Potato Casserole
   - Pair With: Honey-glazed ham, roasted chicken, or cranberry sauce.
   - Presentation: Top with candied pecans or a drizzle of maple syrup for extra flair.
   3. Baked Ham and Scalloped Potatoes
   - Pair With: Steamed green beans, a crisp salad, or warm dinner rolls.
   - Presentation: Serve in a rustic ceramic dish for a homestyle feel.

Creative Twists for Holiday Casseroles

1. Green Bean Casserole with a Twist
   - Add crispy bacon or sautéed mushrooms for added depth.
   - Use almond milk and gluten-free breadcrumbs for a healthier version.
   2. Sweet Potato Casserole Variations
   - Swap marshmallows for a streusel topping made with oats, brown sugar, and butter.
   - Incorporate roasted apples or cranberries for seasonal flavor.
   3. Baked Ham and Scalloped Potatoes
   - Replace ham with smoked turkey or leftover roast beef for a different protein.
   - Add Gruyere or Gouda cheese for a richer, creamier sauce.

Conclusion

Holiday casseroles like Green Bean Casserole, Sweet Potato Casserole, and Baked Ham and Scalloped Potatoes capture the spirit of the season with their comforting flavors and festive presentation. By preparing these dishes ahead of time and following practical tips, you can enjoy a stress-free holiday meal that brings loved ones together. Whether you're hosting a grand feast or a small gathering, these casseroles are sure to impress and create lasting memories around the table. Let these recipes inspire your holiday celebrations and showcase the magic of casseroles as the centerpiece of your festive menu.

Chapter 10: Soups and Stews Transformed into Casseroles

Soups and stews have long been staples of comfort food, warming us on chilly days and nourishing our bodies with hearty, wholesome ingredients. But these dishes don't have to stay in their traditional form. Transforming soups and stews into casseroles brings a new level of texture, depth, and versatility to these beloved meals. With golden crusts, creamy layers, and delightful toppings, these baked dishes offer the same heartiness as their soupy counterparts but with an added element of indulgence. In this chapter, we explore how to turn soups and stews into irresistible casseroles, featuring recipes like Chicken Pot Pie Casserole, French Onion Casserole, and Beef Stew with Biscuit Topping. We'll also provide tips for adding texture and depth to your creations.

Why Transform Soups and Stews into Casseroles?

1. Enhanced Texture

   - Baking soups and stews introduces new textures, from crispy toppings to gooey layers of cheese.

   - Crusts, breadcrumbs, and biscuits add a satisfying crunch or fluffiness that soups alone cannot provide.

   2. Versatility

   - Casseroles can be served as main courses or side dishes.

   - They're easy to customize with your favorite ingredients and toppings.

   3. One-Dish Convenience

   - Casseroles are perfect for feeding a crowd, meal prepping, or minimizing cleanup.

   4. Make-Ahead Friendly

   - Prepare the base (soup or stew) in advance, assemble the casserole, and bake when ready to serve.

Recipe 1: Chicken Pot Pie Casserole

A classic chicken pot pie transforms beautifully into a casserole. This dish combines tender chicken, creamy vegetables, and a flaky crust for the ultimate comfort food.

Ingredients:

- 2 tablespoons unsalted butter
- 1 small onion, diced
- 2 carrots, diced
- 2 celery stalks, diced
- 2 cloves garlic, minced
- 1/4 cup all-purpose flour
- 2 cups chicken broth
- 1/2 cup heavy cream
- 2 cups cooked chicken, shredded
- 1 cup frozen peas
- 1 teaspoon dried thyme
- Salt and pepper to taste
- 1 sheet puff pastry, thawed
- 1 egg, beaten (for egg wash)

Instructions:

1. Preheat oven to 400°F (200°C). Grease a 9x13-inch baking dish.

2. In a large skillet, melt butter over medium heat. Sauté onion, carrots, celery, and garlic until softened, about 5 minutes.

3. Stir in flour and cook for 1–2 minutes. Gradually add chicken broth, whisking constantly, until the mixture thickens. Stir in heavy cream, thyme, salt, and pepper.

4. Add shredded chicken and peas to the sauce. Mix well and transfer to the prepared baking dish.

5. Lay the puff pastry sheet over the casserole, trimming excess edges if needed. Cut small slits to allow steam to escape. Brush with beaten egg.

6. Bake for 25–30 minutes, or until the pastry is golden and flaky. Let cool for 5 minutes before serving.

Tips:

- Substitute puff pastry with homemade pie dough or biscuits for a different texture.

- Add diced potatoes or mushrooms for extra heartiness.

Recipe 2: French Onion Casserole

This casserole takes the rich, caramelized flavors of French onion soup and transforms them into a baked masterpiece, complete with a cheesy, golden topping.

Ingredients:
- 4 large onions, thinly sliced
- 2 tablespoons unsalted butter
- 1 tablespoon olive oil
- 1 teaspoon sugar
- 2 tablespoons all-purpose flour
- 2 cups beef broth
- 1 teaspoon Worcestershire sauce
- 1/2 teaspoon dried thyme
- Salt and pepper to taste
- 1 baguette, sliced into 1-inch pieces
- 2 cups shredded Gruyere cheese

Instructions:

1. Preheat oven to 375°F (190°C). Grease a 9x9-inch baking dish.

2. In a large skillet, heat butter and olive oil over medium heat. Add sliced onions and sugar. Cook, stirring frequently, until the onions are golden and caramelized, about 25–30 minutes.

3. Stir in flour and cook for 1–2 minutes. Gradually add beef broth, Worcestershire sauce, thyme, salt, and pepper. Simmer for 5 minutes.

4. Transfer the onion mixture to the prepared baking dish. Arrange baguette slices on top, slightly overlapping.

5. Sprinkle shredded Gruyere cheese over the baguette slices. Bake for 15–20 minutes, or until the cheese is melted and bubbly. Serve hot.

Tips:
- For a vegetarian version, use vegetable broth instead of beef broth.
- Add a splash of white wine for an extra layer of flavor.

Recipe 3: Beef Stew with Biscuit Topping

Transform a hearty beef stew into a casserole by adding fluffy, golden biscuits on top. This dish is the ultimate in comfort and satisfaction.

Ingredients:

For the Stew:

- 1 lb beef stew meat, cubed
- 2 tablespoons all-purpose flour
- 2 tablespoons olive oil
- 1 small onion, diced
- 2 carrots, diced
- 2 celery stalks, diced
- 2 cups beef broth
- 1 tablespoon tomato paste
- 1 teaspoon dried rosemary
- 1 teaspoon dried thyme
- Salt and pepper to taste

For the Biscuit Topping:

- 1 1/4 cups all-purpose flour
- 1 1/2 teaspoons baking powder
- 1/2 teaspoon salt
- 1/4 cup cold butter, cubed
- 1/2 cup milk

Instructions:

1. Preheat oven to 375°F (190°C). Grease a 9x13-inch baking dish.

2. Toss beef cubes with flour, salt, and pepper. Heat olive oil in a large skillet over medium-high heat. Brown the beef on all sides and set aside.

3. In the same skillet, sauté onion, carrots, and celery until softened, about 5 minutes. Stir in tomato paste, beef broth, rosemary, and thyme. Return the beef to the skillet and simmer for 15 minutes.

4. Transfer the stew to the prepared baking dish.

5. To make the biscuit topping, combine flour, baking powder, and salt in a bowl. Cut in cold butter until the mixture resembles coarse crumbs. Stir in milk until a dough forms. Drop spoonfuls of biscuit dough over the stew.

6. Bake for 20–25 minutes, or until the biscuits are golden and cooked through. Let cool for 5 minutes before serving.

Tips:

- Add peas or green beans to the stew for extra vegetables.

- Substitute the biscuit topping with puff pastry or mashed potatoes.

Creative Ways to Add Texture and Depth

1. Toppings

- Use crispy breadcrumbs, crushed crackers, or grated cheese to add a golden, crunchy finish.

- Incorporate nuts or seeds for a unique twist.

2. Layers

- Layer ingredients like pasta, mashed potatoes, or vegetables to create a visually appealing and flavorful dish.

- Alternate textures, such as creamy sauces with crispy toppings, for contrast.

3. Flavor Boosters

- Use broths, wines, or vinegars to deepen flavors in soups and stews before transforming them into casseroles.

- Add spices and fresh herbs to enhance aromatic notes.

4. Cooking Techniques

- Roast vegetables before adding them to the casserole for a caramelized flavor.

- Sear meats to lock in juices and develop a rich crust.

Conclusion

Transforming soups and stews into casseroles opens up a world of possibilities for creating hearty, comforting, and satisfying dishes. Recipes like Chicken Pot Pie Casserole, French Onion Casserole, and Beef Stew with Biscuit Topping showcase the versatility of these transformations, offering new textures and flavors to enjoy. By experimenting with toppings, layers, and flavor boosters, you can elevate any soup or stew into a show-stopping casserole that will delight your family and guests. Let these recipes inspire your creativity and bring warmth to your table, no matter the season.

Chapter 11: Casseroles with Unique Grains

Casseroles are the ultimate comfort food, combining layers of flavors and textures in a single dish. While staples like pasta and rice often form the foundation of these dishes, incorporating lesser-used grains can elevate your casseroles to a new level of taste, nutrition, and culinary creativity. Grains like farro, millet, and wild rice bring unique flavors and textures that pair beautifully with vegetables, proteins, and creamy sauces. In this chapter, we explore how to use these grains effectively in casseroles, with recipes like Farro and Butternut Squash Bake, Millet and Vegetable Gratin, and Wild Rice and Mushroom Casserole. We also delve into essential cooking techniques to ensure perfect results with these lesser-known grains.

Why Use Unique Grains in Casseroles?

1. Nutritional Benefits

   - Rich in Nutrients: Grains like farro, millet, and wild rice are packed with fiber, protein, and essential vitamins and minerals.

   - Low Glycemic Index: Many of these grains release energy slowly, helping to maintain stable blood sugar levels.

   2. Unique Flavors and Textures

   - Farro: A chewy, nutty grain that holds up well in baking.

   - Millet: A versatile grain with a mild, slightly sweet flavor and a fluffy texture.

   - Wild Rice: Earthy and robust, wild rice adds depth and a satisfying bite to casseroles.

   3. Culinary Creativity

   - Cultural Inspiration: Unique grains allow you to explore global cuisines, from Mediterranean to Asian.

   - Visual Appeal: Their varied colors and shapes make casseroles more visually interesting.

Cooking Techniques for Unfamiliar Grains

1. Rinsing and Soaking

- Rinsing: Remove excess starch or bitterness by rinsing grains under cold water before cooking.

- Soaking: Some grains, like millet and farro, benefit from soaking to reduce cooking time and improve texture.

2. Perfect Water-to-Grain Ratios

- Farro: Use 3 cups of water or broth for every 1 cup of farro. Simmer for 25–30 minutes.

- Millet: Use 2 cups of water for every 1 cup of millet. Cook for 15–20 minutes.

- Wild Rice: Use 3 cups of water for every 1 cup of wild rice. Simmer for 40–50 minutes.

3. Flavor Infusion

- Cook grains in vegetable or chicken broth instead of water for added flavor. Add herbs, spices, or aromatics like garlic and bay leaves to the cooking liquid.

4. Undercooking for Casseroles

- Slightly undercook grains if they'll be baked in a casserole to prevent them from becoming mushy.

Recipe 1: Farro and Butternut Squash Bake

This hearty casserole combines the nutty chewiness of farro with the natural sweetness of roasted butternut squash, creating a dish that's both comforting and nutritious.

Ingredients:
- 1 cup farro, rinsed
- 3 cups vegetable broth
- 2 cups butternut squash, cubed
- 2 tablespoons olive oil
- 1 small onion, diced
- 2 cloves garlic, minced
- 1/2 cup shredded Parmesan cheese
- 1/4 cup chopped fresh parsley
- 1/2 teaspoon dried thyme
- Salt and pepper to taste

Instructions:

1. Preheat oven to 375°F (190°C). Line a baking sheet with parchment paper.

2. Toss butternut squash cubes with 1 tablespoon olive oil, salt, and pepper. Roast for 20–25 minutes, or until tender.

3. In a medium saucepan, cook farro in vegetable broth according to package instructions until slightly undercooked. Drain and set aside.

4. In a skillet, heat the remaining olive oil over medium heat. Sauté onion and garlic until softened, about 3 minutes.

5. In a large mixing bowl, combine cooked farro, roasted butternut squash, onion mixture, Parmesan cheese, parsley, thyme, salt, and pepper. Mix well.

6. Transfer the mixture to a greased 9x9-inch baking dish. Bake for 20–25 minutes, or until heated through. Garnish with additional parsley before serving.

Tips:

- Add toasted walnuts or pecans for extra crunch.

- Substitute sweet potatoes for butternut squash if desired.

Recipe 2: Millet and Vegetable Gratin

This creamy gratin pairs millet's fluffy texture with vibrant vegetables and a cheesy, golden topping. It's a perfect side dish or vegetarian main course.

Ingredients:

- 1 cup millet, rinsed
- 2 cups vegetable broth
- 1 tablespoon olive oil
- 1 cup chopped zucchini
- 1 cup chopped broccoli florets
- 1/2 cup cherry tomatoes, halved
- 1/2 cup shredded mozzarella cheese
- 1/4 cup grated Parmesan cheese
- 1/2 teaspoon garlic powder
- 1/2 teaspoon dried basil
- Salt and pepper to taste

Instructions:

1. Preheat oven to 375°F (190°C). Grease a 9x9-inch baking dish.

2. In a saucepan, cook millet in vegetable broth until slightly undercooked. Fluff with a fork and set aside.

3. In a skillet, heat olive oil over medium heat. Sauté zucchini, broccoli, and cherry tomatoes until tender, about 5 minutes. Season with garlic powder, basil, salt, and pepper.

4. In a large bowl, combine cooked millet, sautéed vegetables, half of the mozzarella, and half of the Parmesan. Mix well.

5. Transfer the mixture to the prepared baking dish. Sprinkle the remaining cheese on top.

6. Bake for 20–25 minutes, or until the cheese is melted and bubbly. Serve hot.

Tips:

- Use dairy-free cheese for a vegan version.

- Add a layer of breadcrumbs mixed with olive oil for a crispy topping.

Recipe 3: Wild Rice and Mushroom Casserole

This earthy casserole highlights the bold flavor of wild rice paired with mushrooms and a creamy, herb-infused sauce.

Ingredients:

- 1 cup wild rice, rinsed
- 3 cups chicken or vegetable broth
- 1 tablespoon butter or olive oil
- 2 cups sliced mushrooms
- 1 small onion, diced
- 2 cloves garlic, minced
- 1/2 cup heavy cream or coconut milk
- 1/2 teaspoon dried thyme
- 1/2 cup grated Gruyere or cheddar cheese (optional)
- Salt and pepper to taste

Instructions:

1. Preheat oven to 375°F (190°C). Grease a 9x9-inch baking dish.

2. Cook wild rice in chicken or vegetable broth until slightly undercooked. Drain and set aside.

3. In a skillet, melt butter over medium heat. Sauté mushrooms, onion, and garlic until softened, about 5 minutes. Season with thyme, salt, and pepper.

4. In a mixing bowl, combine cooked wild rice, mushroom mixture, and heavy cream. Stir until evenly combined.

5. Transfer the mixture to the prepared baking dish. Sprinkle Gruyere or cheddar cheese on top, if using.

6. Bake for 25–30 minutes, or until heated through and bubbly. Let cool for 5 minutes before serving.

Tips:

- Add cooked chicken or turkey for a heartier dish.

- Incorporate spinach or kale for extra greens.

Creative Variations for Unique Grains

1. Mediterranean Farro Bake

- Add sun-dried tomatoes, Kalamata olives, and feta cheese to the farro mixture.

2. Curried Millet Casserole

- Season millet with curry powder and add roasted cauliflower and chickpeas.

3. Wild Rice Stuffed Peppers

- Use wild rice casserole as a filling for bell peppers, then bake until tender.

Conclusion

Casseroles with unique grains like farro, millet, and wild rice bring exciting flavors, textures, and nutritional benefits to your table. Recipes like Farro and Butternut Squash Bake, Millet and Vegetable Gratin, and Wild Rice and Mushroom Casserole showcase how these grains can transform traditional casseroles into culinary masterpieces. With the right cooking techniques and a touch of creativity, you can explore new possibilities and enjoy the wholesome satisfaction of these lesser-used grains in your favorite comfort food format. Let these recipes inspire you to embrace the versatility of grains and elevate your casserole game.

Chapter 12: Seafood Casseroles

Seafood casseroles bring an element of elegance and indulgence to comforting baked dishes. They combine the rich flavors of the sea with creamy sauces, hearty grains, and savory toppings, making them perfect for special occasions or as a standout weeknight meal. Whether you're savoring a Southern-inspired Shrimp and Grits Casserole, indulging in a decadent Lobster Mac and Cheese, or enjoying the fresh flavors of a Salmon and Dill Potato Bake, seafood casseroles showcase the versatility and sophistication of these oceanic delights. This chapter explores these recipes, along with tips for handling and cooking seafood to ensure perfect results every time.

Why Seafood Casseroles?

1. Elevated Comfort Food

Seafood casseroles combine the warmth and heartiness of classic casseroles with the luxurious flavors of seafood.

2. Nutritional Benefits

- High in Protein: Seafood is an excellent source of lean protein.

- Omega-3 Fatty Acids: Many types of seafood, like salmon, are rich in heart-healthy fats.

3. Versatility

- Variety of Flavors: From delicate shrimp to rich lobster, seafood pairs beautifully with creamy, cheesy, and herbed casseroles.

- Adaptability: Recipes can be adjusted to accommodate different types of seafood and ingredients.

Tips for Handling and Cooking Seafood in Casseroles

1. Choose Fresh or High-Quality Frozen Seafood

- Fresh Seafood: Look for clear, firm flesh and a mild ocean scent. Avoid any seafood that smells "fishy."

- Frozen Seafood: Choose vacuum-sealed, flash-frozen seafood to preserve freshness.

2. Thaw Properly

- Thaw frozen seafood in the refrigerator overnight or under cold running water. Avoid thawing at room temperature to prevent bacterial growth.

3. Pre-Cook When Necessary

- To prevent overcooking, pre-cook seafood lightly before adding it to casseroles. This ensures it will be perfectly tender after baking.

4. Enhance Flavor

- Marinate seafood with lemon juice, garlic, or herbs to enhance its natural flavors.

5. Avoid Overcooking

- Most seafood cooks quickly, so adjust baking times accordingly to prevent a rubbery texture.

Recipe 1: Shrimp and Grits Casserole

This Southern-inspired dish combines creamy grits with tender shrimp, cheddar cheese, and a touch of spice for a casserole that's comforting and full of flavor.

Ingredients:
- 1 cup stone-ground grits
- 4 cups chicken or vegetable broth
- 1/2 cup heavy cream
- 1 cup shredded cheddar cheese
- 1 tablespoon butter
- 1 lb shrimp, peeled and deveined
- 1 small onion, diced
- 2 cloves garlic, minced
- 1/2 teaspoon smoked paprika
- 1/4 teaspoon cayenne pepper (optional)
- Salt and pepper to taste
- 1/4 cup chopped green onions (for garnish)

Instructions:

1. Preheat oven to 375°F (190°C). Grease a 9x9-inch baking dish.

2. In a saucepan, bring chicken broth to a boil. Gradually whisk in grits, reduce heat, and simmer until thickened, about 20 minutes. Stir in heavy cream, cheddar cheese, and butter. Season with salt and pepper.

3. In a skillet, heat olive oil over medium heat. Sauté onion and garlic until softened. Add shrimp, paprika, cayenne pepper, salt, and pepper. Cook until shrimp are pink and just cooked through, about 3 minutes.

4. Fold the shrimp mixture into the grits. Transfer the mixture to the prepared baking dish.

5. Bake for 20–25 minutes, or until the casserole is set and bubbly. Garnish with chopped green onions before serving.

Tips:

- Substitute gouda or Monterey Jack for a different cheese profile.

- Add cooked bacon or sausage for extra flavor.

Recipe 2: Lobster Mac and Cheese

Rich, creamy, and indulgent, Lobster Mac and Cheese is a decadent take on a comfort food classic. It's perfect for holidays, celebrations, or any time you want to treat yourself.

Ingredients:

- 1 lb elbow macaroni or cavatappi pasta
- 2 tablespoons butter
- 2 tablespoons all-purpose flour
- 2 cups whole milk
- 1/2 cup heavy cream
- 2 cups shredded cheddar cheese
- 1 cup shredded Gruyere cheese
- 1/4 cup grated Parmesan cheese
- 1/2 teaspoon garlic powder
- Salt and pepper to taste
- 1 lb cooked lobster meat, chopped
- 1/2 cup panko breadcrumbs
- 1 tablespoon olive oil

Instructions:

1. Preheat oven to 375°F (190°C). Grease a 9x13-inch baking dish.

2. Cook pasta according to package instructions until al dente. Drain and set aside.

3. In a saucepan, melt butter over medium heat. Whisk in flour and cook for 1 minute. Gradually add milk and heavy cream, whisking constantly until thickened.

4. Stir in cheddar, Gruyere, Parmesan, garlic powder, salt, and pepper. Mix until the cheese is melted and the sauce is smooth.

5. Combine the cheese sauce, cooked pasta, and lobster meat in a large bowl. Transfer to the prepared baking dish.

6. In a small bowl, toss panko breadcrumbs with olive oil. Sprinkle over the casserole.

7. Bake for 20–25 minutes, or until the top is golden and bubbly. Let cool for 5 minutes before serving.

Tips:

- Replace lobster with crab or shrimp for a different twist.

- Add a pinch of nutmeg to the cheese sauce for a subtle depth of flavor.

Recipe 3: Salmon and Dill Potato Bake

This casserole combines tender salmon, creamy potatoes, and fresh dill for a light yet satisfying dish that's full of fresh flavors.

Ingredients:

- 1 lb Yukon Gold potatoes, thinly sliced

- 1 tablespoon olive oil

- 1 lb fresh salmon fillets, skin removed

- 1/2 cup sour cream

- 1/2 cup heavy cream

- 2 tablespoons Dijon mustard

- 2 tablespoons fresh dill, chopped

- 1/2 teaspoon garlic powder

- Salt and pepper to taste

- 1/2 cup shredded Gruyere or Swiss cheese (optional)

Instructions:

1. Preheat oven to 375°F (190°C). Grease a 9x13-inch baking dish.

2. Toss potato slices with olive oil, garlic powder, salt, and pepper. Arrange half of the potatoes in the bottom of the baking dish.

3. Season salmon fillets with salt and pepper. Place the salmon on top of the potatoes.

4. In a bowl, whisk together sour cream, heavy cream, Dijon mustard, and dill. Pour the mixture over the salmon and potatoes.

5. Arrange the remaining potato slices on top. Sprinkle with shredded cheese, if using.

6. Cover with foil and bake for 25 minutes. Remove foil and bake for an additional 15 minutes, or until the potatoes are tender and the top is golden. Let cool for 5 minutes before serving.

Tips:

- Substitute salmon with cod or haddock if desired.

- Serve with a side of steamed asparagus or green beans for a complete meal.

Creative Variations for Seafood Casseroles

1. Shrimp Scampi Casserole

- Toss cooked shrimp with linguine, garlic butter, lemon juice, and parsley. Top with breadcrumbs and bake.

2. Crab and Spinach Casserole

- Combine crab meat with sautéed spinach, cream cheese, and Parmesan for a rich, savory bake.

3. Seafood Paella Bake

- Mix seafood like mussels, shrimp, and clams with saffron-seasoned rice and bake until golden.

Conclusion

Seafood casseroles like Shrimp and Grits Casserole, Lobster Mac and Cheese, and Salmon and Dill Potato Bake combine the best of comforting casseroles with the elegance of fresh seafood. These dishes showcase the versatility and rich flavors of seafood while offering a range of textures and culinary experiences. By following tips for handling and cooking seafood, you can create perfectly balanced casseroles that will impress family and guests alike.

Let these recipes inspire you to bring the flavors of the ocean to your table, turning any meal into a memorable occasion.

Chapter 13: Freezer-Friendly Casseroles

Freezer-friendly casseroles are the unsung heroes of meal prepping and gifting. They're perfect for busy weeknights, helping loved ones during challenging times, or simply ensuring a hearty meal is always within reach. These casseroles are designed to be made in advance, stored in the freezer, and reheated whenever needed, all while maintaining their flavor and texture. In this chapter, we'll explore the art of freezer-friendly casseroles with recipes for Make-Ahead Baked Ziti, Frozen Breakfast Strata, and Chicken Enchilada Bake. Additionally, we'll provide best practices for freezing, thawing, and reheating casseroles to guarantee perfect results every time.

The Appeal of Freezer-Friendly Casseroles

1. Convenience and Time-Saving
   - Make-Ahead Meals: Spend less time cooking on busy days by preparing casseroles in advance.
   - Batch Cooking: Prepare multiple casseroles in one go to stock the freezer for weeks.
   2. Perfect for Gifting
   - Helping Hands: Freezer casseroles are a thoughtful gift for new parents, friends recovering from illness, or anyone needing a little extra support.
   3. Reduced Food Waste
   - Preserve Ingredients: Freezing casseroles prevents food from going bad before it's cooked.
   - Portion Control: Freeze individual portions for easy, waste-free meals.

Best Practices for Freezing, Thawing, and Reheating Casseroles

1. Preparing for the Freezer
   - Choose the Right Dish: Use freezer-safe containers like aluminum pans, glass dishes with lids, or heavy-duty plastic containers.

- Wrap It Well: Cover the casserole tightly with plastic wrap, foil, or a lid to prevent freezer burn.

- Label Clearly: Include the casserole name, date, and reheating instructions on the package.

2. Freezing Tips

- Cool Completely: Allow casseroles to cool completely before freezing to prevent condensation and ice crystals.

- Skip the Topping: Add crunchy toppings like breadcrumbs or cheese just before baking to maintain texture.

- Freeze Flat: For liquid-based casseroles, freeze them flat in freezer bags for easier storage.

3. Thawing and Reheating

- Thaw Safely: Thaw casseroles in the refrigerator overnight or use the defrost setting on a microwave. Avoid thawing at room temperature.

- Reheat Gradually: Reheat casseroles in a 350°F (175°C) oven, covered, until heated through. Add toppings and bake uncovered for the final 10–15 minutes.

- Check for Doneness: Ensure casseroles are heated to an internal temperature of 165°F (74°C).

Recipe 1: Make-Ahead Baked Ziti

This classic Italian-American casserole is the ultimate comfort food, and it freezes beautifully. With layers of pasta, marinara, cheese, and ground beef, it's perfect for any occasion.

Ingredients:

- 1 lb ziti or penne pasta
- 1 lb ground beef or Italian sausage
- 1 jar (24 oz) marinara sauce
- 1 cup ricotta cheese
- 1/2 cup grated Parmesan cheese
- 2 cups shredded mozzarella cheese
- 1 teaspoon garlic powder
- 1 teaspoon dried oregano
- Salt and pepper to taste

Instructions:

1. Preheat oven to 375°F (190°C) if baking immediately. Grease a 9x13-inch baking dish.

2. Cook pasta according to package instructions until al dente. Drain and set aside.

3. In a skillet, cook ground beef over medium heat until browned. Drain excess fat and stir in marinara sauce, garlic powder, oregano, salt, and pepper. Simmer for 5 minutes.

4. In a large mixing bowl, combine cooked pasta, meat sauce, ricotta, Parmesan, and half of the mozzarella. Mix until evenly coated.

5. Transfer the mixture to the prepared baking dish. Top with remaining mozzarella.

6. To Freeze: Cool completely, wrap tightly, and freeze.

7. To Bake: Thaw overnight in the refrigerator. Bake at 375°F (190°C) for 30–35 minutes, or until bubbly and golden.

Tips:
- Add spinach or mushrooms for extra vegetables.
- Use plant-based ground meat for a vegetarian version.

Recipe 2: Frozen Breakfast Strata

This make-ahead breakfast casserole is packed with eggs, bread, cheese, and vegetables, making it a perfect freezer-friendly option for busy mornings or holiday brunches.

Ingredients:
- 6 large eggs
- 2 cups milk
- 1 teaspoon Dijon mustard
- 1/2 teaspoon salt
- 1/4 teaspoon black pepper
- 4 cups cubed bread (French or sourdough)
- 1 cup shredded cheddar cheese
- 1/2 cup diced ham or cooked sausage (optional)
- 1 cup chopped spinach or broccoli
- 1/2 cup diced bell peppers

Instructions:

1. Grease a 9x9-inch baking dish.

2. In a large bowl, whisk together eggs, milk, Dijon mustard, salt, and pepper.

3. Add cubed bread, cheese, meat (if using), and vegetables to the egg mixture. Stir until well combined.

4. Transfer the mixture to the prepared baking dish.

5. To Freeze: Cover tightly with plastic wrap and foil. Freeze.

6. To Bake: Thaw overnight in the refrigerator. Bake at 375°F (190°C) for 40–45 minutes, or until the top is golden and the center is set.

Tips:

- Substitute plant-based sausage or tofu for a vegetarian version.

- Add chopped sun-dried tomatoes or feta for a Mediterranean twist.

Recipe 3: Chicken Enchilada Bake

This flavorful casserole features layers of tortillas, shredded chicken, enchilada sauce, and cheese for a Tex-Mex-inspired dish that's easy to prepare and freeze.

Ingredients:

- 2 cups cooked shredded chicken

- 1 can (15 oz) enchilada sauce

- 1 cup sour cream

- 1 teaspoon cumin

- 1/2 teaspoon chili powder

- 8 small flour or corn tortillas

- 2 cups shredded cheddar or Monterey Jack cheese

- 1/4 cup chopped cilantro (for garnish)

Instructions:

1. Preheat oven to 375°F (190°C) if baking immediately. Grease a 9x13-inch baking dish.

2. In a large bowl, combine shredded chicken, sour cream, cumin, chili powder, and half of the enchilada sauce.

3. Spread a thin layer of enchilada sauce on the bottom of the baking dish. Layer tortillas, chicken mixture, and cheese, repeating until all ingredients are used. End with a layer of cheese on top.

4. To Freeze: Cool completely, wrap tightly, and freeze.

5. To Bake: Thaw overnight in the refrigerator. Bake at 375°F (190°C) for 25–30 minutes, or until bubbly and golden. Garnish with cilantro before serving.

Tips:

- Add black beans or corn for extra texture and flavor.

- Serve with guacamole, salsa, or sour cream.

Creative Freezer-Friendly Casserole Variations

1. Vegetarian Lasagna

- Use layers of zucchini or eggplant in place of pasta, along with ricotta, marinara, and mozzarella.

2. Shepherd's Pie

- Combine ground turkey or lentils with vegetables and gravy, topped with mashed potatoes.

3. Broccoli and Rice Casserole

- Mix cooked rice, steamed broccoli, shredded chicken, and a creamy cheese sauce.

Conclusion

Freezer-friendly casseroles like Make-Ahead Baked Ziti, Frozen Breakfast Strata, and Chicken Enchilada Bake are a game-changer for meal prep and gifting. These versatile dishes simplify busy schedules while ensuring delicious, home-cooked meals are always on hand. By mastering the art of freezing, thawing, and reheating casseroles, you can create satisfying meals that retain their flavor and texture, even after weeks in the freezer. Let these recipes inspire you to stock your freezer with comforting casseroles that are ready to be enjoyed at a moment's notice.

Chapter 14: Decadent Dessert Casseroles

Dessert casseroles are the perfect marriage of comfort food and indulgence, bringing the warmth and satisfaction of a traditional casserole to the sweeter side of the table. They are versatile, crowd-pleasing, and easy to make, making them ideal for holidays, gatherings, or simply treating yourself after a long day. From the classic southern charm of Peach Cobbler Casserole to the rich, chocolatey depths of Bread Pudding and the comforting crunch of Apple Crisp Bake, these dishes celebrate sweetness in every bite. This chapter explores these decadent dessert casseroles, showcasing how to incorporate seasonal fruits and ingredients to maximize flavor and satisfaction.

The Allure of Dessert Casseroles

1. Comforting and Nostalgic
   - Warm and Familiar: These desserts evoke feelings of nostalgia with their warm, gooey textures and homestyle flavors.
   - Simple yet Elegant: Perfect for casual family dinners or as the grand finale to a dinner party.
   2. Crowd-Pleasing Appeal
   - Feeding a Group: Large-format desserts are ideal for serving a crowd, eliminating the need for individual portions.
   - Customizable: Adjust ingredients to suit dietary preferences or seasonal availability.
   3. Seasonal Versatility
   - Fresh Fruits: Highlight the best of each season, from juicy summer peaches to crisp autumn apples.
   - Rich Ingredients: Incorporate spices, chocolate, and nuts for added depth.

Tips for Creating Perfect Dessert Casseroles

1. Use Quality Ingredients

- Opt for fresh, in-season fruits and high-quality chocolate, butter, and dairy for the best results.

2. Balance Textures

- Pair soft fillings with crunchy toppings like streusel, nuts, or caramelized crusts to create contrast.

3. Adjust Sweetness

- Taste as you go, especially when working with fruits. Add sugar sparingly to balance natural sweetness without overpowering flavors.

4. Serve Warm

- Dessert casseroles are best served warm, often straight from the oven, with a dollop of whipped cream or a scoop of vanilla ice cream.

Recipe 1: Peach Cobbler Casserole

A beloved Southern classic, Peach Cobbler Casserole combines sweet, juicy peaches with a buttery, golden biscuit topping for a dessert that's as comforting as it is delicious.

Ingredients:

- 6 cups fresh peaches, peeled and sliced (or 2 cans, drained)
- 1/2 cup granulated sugar
- 1/4 cup brown sugar
- 1 teaspoon cinnamon
- 1/4 teaspoon nutmeg
- 1 tablespoon cornstarch
- 1 teaspoon vanilla extract
- 1 cup all-purpose flour
- 1/4 cup granulated sugar
- 1 teaspoon baking powder
- 1/4 teaspoon salt
- 1/2 cup unsalted butter, cold and cubed
- 1/2 cup buttermilk

Instructions:

1. Preheat oven to 375°F (190°C). Grease a 9x13-inch baking dish.

2. In a large mixing bowl, toss peaches with granulated sugar, brown sugar, cinnamon, nutmeg, cornstarch, and vanilla extract. Spread evenly in the prepared baking dish.

3. In another bowl, whisk together flour, sugar, baking powder, and salt. Cut in butter with a pastry cutter until the mixture resembles coarse crumbs. Stir in buttermilk until just combined.

4. Drop spoonfuls of the biscuit mixture over the peaches. Spread gently to cover most of the filling.

5. Bake for 35–40 minutes, or until the topping is golden and the peaches are bubbling. Let cool slightly before serving.

Tips:

- Substitute peaches with nectarines, apricots, or plums for a seasonal variation.

- Add a sprinkle of chopped pecans or almonds to the topping for extra crunch.

Recipe 2: Chocolate Bread Pudding

Chocolate Bread Pudding is a rich, decadent dessert that transforms day-old bread into a luscious, custard-soaked treat with layers of melted chocolate.

Ingredients:
- 6 cups cubed bread (challah, brioche, or French bread)
- 2 cups whole milk
- 1 cup heavy cream
- 1/2 cup granulated sugar
- 1/4 cup brown sugar
- 4 large eggs
- 1 teaspoon vanilla extract
- 1/2 teaspoon cinnamon
- 1/4 teaspoon salt
- 1 cup semi-sweet chocolate chips
- Powdered sugar (for garnish)

Instructions:
1. Preheat oven to 350°F (175°C). Grease a 9x9-inch baking dish.
2. Arrange bread cubes in the prepared dish.

3. In a medium saucepan, heat milk, cream, granulated sugar, and brown sugar over medium heat until warm. Remove from heat.

4. In a large bowl, whisk eggs, vanilla extract, cinnamon, and salt. Gradually whisk in the warm milk mixture.

5. Pour the custard evenly over the bread cubes, pressing gently to ensure all pieces are soaked. Sprinkle chocolate chips on top.

6. Bake for 35–40 minutes, or until the custard is set and the top is slightly crisp. Let cool for 10 minutes before dusting with powdered sugar.

Tips:

- Add a splash of bourbon or coffee liqueur to the custard for a flavor boost.

- Serve with whipped cream or vanilla ice cream for an indulgent finish.

Recipe 3: Apple Crisp Bake

Apple Crisp Bake is a quintessential autumn dessert that combines tender, cinnamon-spiced apples with a crunchy oat and brown sugar topping.

Ingredients:

- 6 cups apples, peeled and sliced (Granny Smith or Honeycrisp recommended)

- 1/4 cup granulated sugar

- 1/4 cup brown sugar

- 1 teaspoon cinnamon

- 1/4 teaspoon nutmeg

- 1 tablespoon lemon juice

- 1 tablespoon cornstarch

- 1 cup rolled oats

- 1/2 cup all-purpose flour

- 1/2 cup brown sugar

- 1/2 teaspoon cinnamon

- 1/4 teaspoon salt

- 1/2 cup unsalted butter, melted

Instructions:

1. Preheat oven to 375°F (190°C). Grease a 9x9-inch baking dish.

2. In a large bowl, toss apples with granulated sugar, brown sugar, cinnamon, nutmeg, lemon juice, and cornstarch. Spread evenly in the baking dish.

3. In a separate bowl, combine oats, flour, brown sugar, cinnamon, and salt. Stir in melted butter until the mixture forms coarse crumbs. Sprinkle evenly over the apples.

4. Bake for 35–40 minutes, or until the topping is golden and the apples are tender. Let cool slightly before serving.

Tips:

- Add chopped walnuts or pecans to the topping for extra crunch.

- Serve with caramel sauce and vanilla ice cream for a decadent finish.

Incorporating Seasonal Fruits and Ingredients

1. Spring
   - Highlight berries like strawberries, raspberries, and blueberries.
   - Add a splash of citrus, such as lemon or orange zest, to brighten flavors.
2. Summer
   - Use stone fruits like peaches, plums, and cherries.
   - Pair fruits with herbs like basil or mint for a fresh twist.
3. Autumn
   - Focus on apples, pears, and pumpkins.
   - Incorporate warming spices like cinnamon, nutmeg, and cloves.
4. Winter
   - Use frozen fruits like berries or mangoes when fresh options are limited.
   - Combine chocolate with spices like cardamom or ginger for cozy flavors.

Conclusion

Decadent dessert casseroles like Peach Cobbler Casserole, Chocolate Bread Pudding, and Apple Crisp Bake are the epitome of comfort and indulgence. By incorporating seasonal fruits and high-quality ingredients, these recipes deliver maximum flavor and satisfaction. Whether served warm with a scoop of ice cream or as a standalone treat, dessert casseroles bring joy to every gathering and celebration. Let these recipes inspire your next sweet creation, ensuring that your table is always filled with warmth and sweetness.

Chapter 15: Tips, Tricks, and Variations

Casseroles are a cornerstone of home cooking, offering endless opportunities for creativity, comfort, and convenience. However, crafting the perfect casserole isn't always as simple as tossing ingredients together and baking. From achieving ideal textures to adapting recipes for dietary needs, there are countless ways to elevate your casserole game. This chapter provides expert tips, tricks, and variations to ensure your casseroles are always a hit. We'll tackle common challenges, explore the art of layering flavors and textures, and share strategies for customizing casseroles to suit any dietary preference or ingredient availability.

Common Casserole Challenges and How to Overcome Them

1. Soggy Textures

Problem: Casseroles can become watery due to excess liquid from vegetables or improper layering.

Solutions:

- Pre-Cook Vegetables: Sauté or roast vegetables like zucchini, mushrooms, or spinach to remove excess moisture before adding them to your casserole.

- Use a Thickener: Incorporate a roux, cornstarch slurry, or creamy sauce to bind ingredients and absorb excess liquid.

- Drain Canned Ingredients: Always drain and rinse canned beans, vegetables, or tuna to reduce added moisture.

2. Overcooked or Undercooked Layers

Problem: Different components of the casserole may cook at varying rates, leading to uneven results.

Solutions:

- Par-Cook Ingredients: Partially cook proteins like chicken or ground beef and starches like pasta or rice before assembling.

- Cut Ingredients Evenly: Uniformly sized pieces ensure even cooking.

3. Bland Flavors

Problem: Casseroles can taste flat if not properly seasoned.

Solutions:

- Layer Seasonings: Season each component separately—proteins, vegetables, and sauces.

- Add Bold Ingredients: Use sharp cheeses, cured meats, or aromatic herbs to enhance flavor.

- Boost with Acidity: Add a splash of lemon juice, vinegar, or wine to brighten the overall flavor.

4. Overly Dry Casseroles

Problem: Casseroles may dry out if there isn't enough moisture or if they're overbaked.

Solutions:

- Cover During Baking: Use foil to retain moisture and remove it during the last 10–15 minutes for browning.

- Add a Sauce: Ensure there's a balance of creamy or liquid components like béchamel, marinara, or broth.

Layering Flavors and Textures for the Perfect Bake

1. Building the Base

- Start with a sturdy layer to provide structure and soak up flavors, such as cooked pasta, rice, or thinly sliced potatoes.

- For crust-based casseroles, use a pre-baked pie crust, puff pastry, or crushed crackers.

2. Adding Protein

- Spread an even layer of pre-cooked proteins like shredded chicken, ground beef, or tofu.

- Incorporate plant-based proteins like lentils, beans, or chickpeas for vegetarian options.

3. Vegetables for Flavor and Nutrition

- Use a combination of roasted, steamed, or sautéed vegetables to add depth and color.

- Layer softer vegetables like spinach or zucchini above firmer ones like carrots or broccoli to ensure even cooking.

4. Creamy or Saucy Layers

- Spread a flavorful sauce, such as béchamel, marinara, or a creamy cheese sauce, between layers to bind ingredients.

- For dairy-free options, use coconut milk, cashew cream, or a blended vegetable sauce like butternut squash.

5. Topping It Off

- Add a finishing layer for texture and visual appeal. Options include:

- Cheese: Shredded cheddar, mozzarella, or Parmesan for a gooey, golden crust.

- Breadcrumbs: Combine with butter or olive oil for a crispy, crunchy topping.

- Nuts or Seeds: Chopped almonds, pecans, or sunflower seeds add a unique crunch.

Adapting Recipes for Dietary Needs or Ingredient Availability

1. Gluten-Free

- Substitute Starches: Replace pasta with gluten-free alternatives like rice noodles or spiralized zucchini.

- Thicken Without Flour: Use cornstarch, arrowroot, or gluten-free all-purpose flour for sauces.

2. Dairy-Free

- Swap Cheeses: Use dairy-free cheese or nutritional yeast for a cheesy flavor.

- Create Creamy Sauces: Blend soaked cashews, silken tofu, or coconut milk for rich, dairy-free sauces.

3. Vegetarian and Vegan

- Protein Replacements: Substitute meat with lentils, chickpeas, or crumbled tofu.

- Flavor Enhancers: Use umami-rich ingredients like mushrooms, miso paste, or smoked paprika to add depth.

4. Low-Carb or Keto

- Replace Starches: Use cauliflower rice, spaghetti squash, or thinly sliced zucchini instead of pasta or rice.

- Focus on Fats: Incorporate high-fat, low-carb ingredients like cheese, cream, and avocado.

5. Ingredient Swaps for Availability

- Seasonal Vegetables: Adjust recipes to feature what's in season—substitute asparagus for green beans in spring or butternut squash for sweet potatoes in fall.

- Flexible Proteins: Use whatever protein you have on hand, like swapping ground turkey for beef or canned tuna for chicken.

Creative Casserole Variations

1. Global Flavors

- Mexican-Inspired: Layer tortillas with enchilada sauce, black beans, and shredded cheese for a Tex-Mex twist.

- Mediterranean Style: Combine orzo, roasted vegetables, feta, and a lemon-dill sauce.

- Asian Fusion: Use rice noodles, sautéed vegetables, and a soy-ginger sauce with shredded chicken or tofu.

2. Breakfast Casseroles

- Sweet Options: Make a baked French toast casserole with brioche, eggs, and cinnamon.

- Savory Choices: Combine hash browns, eggs, cheese, and sausage for a hearty breakfast bake.

3. Dessert Casseroles

- Classic Cobbler: Top seasonal fruit with a biscuit or streusel topping.

- Bread Pudding: Use day-old bread with a custard base and flavorings like vanilla, chocolate, or caramel.

4. Single-Serving Casseroles

- Use ramekins or small baking dishes to create individualized portions. Perfect for customizing to different dietary needs or preferences.

Elevating Your Casserole Game

1. Experiment with Spices
   - Use spice blends like Italian seasoning, Cajun spices, or garam masala to add flair.
   2. Garnish for Impact
   - Add fresh herbs, a drizzle of balsamic glaze, or a sprinkle of lemon zest after baking for a finishing touch.
   3. Play with Presentation
   - Layer ingredients visually in clear dishes to showcase colorful layers.
   - Serve casseroles in cast iron skillets or rustic ceramic dishes for a homestyle feel.
   4. Make It Interactive
   - Allow guests to build their own casseroles with pre-prepped components, such as a DIY lasagna bar or taco casserole station.

Conclusion

Mastering casseroles requires a balance of flavors, textures, and thoughtful adaptations to suit different tastes and dietary needs. By addressing common challenges, layering ingredients strategically, and exploring creative variations, you can elevate any casserole from ordinary to extraordinary. Whether you're feeding a family, impressing guests, or repurposing pantry staples, these tips, tricks, and variations ensure that your casseroles are always a crowd-pleaser. Let this chapter be your guide to turning every bake into a culinary triumph.

Conclusion: Celebrating the Art of Casseroles

Casseroles hold a unique and enduring place in culinary tradition, bridging the gap between comfort and creativity. They're the epitome of home cooking—versatile, accessible, and endlessly customizable. From hearty weeknight dinners to show-stopping holiday feasts, casseroles offer a dish for every occasion and satisfy the cravings of all ages. This final chapter reflects on the charm and versatility of casseroles, encourages you to experiment and make each recipe your own, and provides resources for further inspiration in your culinary journey.

The Timeless Appeal of Casseroles

1. Comfort and Nostalgia

Casseroles evoke memories of family gatherings, potluck dinners, and cherished traditions. Their warm, satisfying nature connects generations and cultures, making them a universal symbol of togetherness.

2. Versatility in Every Bite

- Global Influences: From Italian lasagnas to Mexican enchiladas, casseroles adapt seamlessly to a variety of cuisines.

- Seasonal Flexibility: Whether it's a summer veggie bake or a hearty winter stew, casseroles celebrate the flavors of every season.

3. Simplicity and Convenience

- One-Dish Wonders: Combining proteins, vegetables, and grains into a single dish simplifies meal preparation and cleanup.

- Make-Ahead Magic: Many casseroles can be prepared in advance, frozen, and baked when needed, making them perfect for busy lifestyles.

Encouragement to Experiment

Casseroles are a canvas for culinary creativity. The recipes shared in this book are just the beginning—each can be adapted, reimagined, or reinvented to suit your tastes, dietary needs, or available ingredients.

1. Personalizing Recipes

- Swap Ingredients: Replace proteins, grains, or vegetables based on what you have on hand. For example, substitute quinoa for rice or tofu for chicken.

- Adjust Flavors: Add your favorite spices, herbs, or condiments to customize the dish to your liking.

2. Incorporating Family Traditions

- Revive a family recipe or adapt a cultural dish into a casserole format. For example, transform classic shepherd's pie with a twist by adding global spices or alternative toppings.

3. Embracing Imperfection

- Cooking is an art, not a science. If your first attempt isn't perfect, use it as an opportunity to learn and improve. Experimentation often leads to the most exciting discoveries.

4. Engaging the Family

- Turn casserole-making into a collaborative activity by involving family members. Let children layer ingredients, choose toppings, or name their creation.

Casseroles for Every Occasion

Casseroles shine in their ability to cater to diverse settings, whether you're hosting a dinner party, preparing a quick weeknight meal, or celebrating a special event. Here are a few ideas for incorporating casseroles into your routine:

1. Weeknight Dinners

- Opt for quick and easy casseroles like Taco Casserole or One-Pot Pasta Bake.

- Use leftovers creatively to reduce waste and save time.

2. Entertaining

- Impress guests with sophisticated casseroles like Lobster Mac and Cheese or Mediterranean Vegetable Bake.

- Prepare casseroles in advance, allowing you to focus on hosting.

3. Holidays and Celebrations

- Highlight casseroles as the star of the feast with recipes like Baked Ham and Scalloped Potatoes or Sweet Potato Casserole.

- Include dessert casseroles like Apple Crisp Bake for a sweet finale.

4. Gifting
- Share the comfort of casseroles with friends or neighbors during life's milestones, such as welcoming a new baby, recovering from illness, or celebrating achievements.

Resources for Further Culinary Exploration

1. Online Recipe Platforms

Websites like AllRecipes, Food Network, and Epicurious offer thousands of casserole recipes from around the world. Use them as inspiration to discover new flavors and techniques.

2. Cookbooks

Expand your culinary library with cookbooks dedicated to casseroles, comfort food, or specific cuisines. Some recommendations include:
- *The Casserole Queens Cookbook* by Crystal Cook and Sandy Pollock.
- *The Complete Comfort Food Cookbook* by America's Test Kitchen.

3. Social Media and Blogs

Follow food bloggers and social media accounts specializing in casseroles or home cooking. Platforms like Instagram, Pinterest, and YouTube are brimming with tutorials and creative ideas.

4. Local Cooking Classes

Join community cooking classes to learn new techniques, meet fellow food enthusiasts, and gain hands-on experience. Many classes focus on comfort food or specific cuisines.

5. Food Markets and Farms

Explore local farmers' markets or community-supported agriculture (CSA) programs to find fresh, seasonal ingredients for your casseroles.

A Few Final Tips for Casserole Success

1. Keep It Balanced

Strive for harmony in your casseroles by balancing textures (creamy vs. crunchy) and flavors (savory vs. tangy).

2. Prioritize Freshness

- Use high-quality ingredients, especially for fresh vegetables, cheeses, and proteins.

- Opt for seasonal produce whenever possible for peak flavor.

3. Invest in Quality Bakeware

- Choose durable, oven-safe dishes made of glass, ceramic, or cast iron for even cooking and easy cleanup.

- Consider portion-sized ramekins or smaller dishes for individual servings.

4. Document Your Creations

- Keep a cooking journal to record your favorite recipes, adaptations, and feedback from family or guests.

- Photograph your casseroles and share them with friends or on social media for inspiration.

Reflecting on the Journey

This book has taken you on a culinary journey through the world of casseroles, from breakfast bakes to freezer-friendly dinners and decadent desserts. Along the way, you've learned how to:

- Transform simple ingredients into satisfying one-dish meals.

- Adapt recipes to suit a variety of tastes, dietary needs, and occasions.

- Master techniques to overcome common challenges and elevate flavors.

Casseroles are more than just recipes—they are expressions of love, warmth, and creativity. Each dish you prepare tells a story, whether it's a family recipe passed down through generations or an experiment that becomes a new favorite.

A Final Word of Encouragement

Don't be afraid to take risks, try new ingredients, and embrace the unexpected. Cooking is a journey, and casseroles offer endless opportunities to explore, create, and connect with others through food. Let this book serve as your foundation, but don't hesitate to push boundaries and make each recipe uniquely yours.

From weeknight dinners to festive celebrations, casseroles have a place at every table. They remind us that cooking is not just about feeding the body but also nourishing the soul. So, preheat your oven, gather your ingredients, and let the joy of casserole-making fill your kitchen.

Happy cooking, and may your casseroles always be a source of comfort, creativity, and connection.

Don't miss out!

Visit the website below and you can sign up to receive emails whenever Olivia Bennett publishes a new book. There's no charge and no obligation.

https://books2read.com/r/B-A-QLEKD-SHQAG

BOOKS2READ

Connecting independent readers to independent writers.

About the Author

Olivia Bennett is a celebrated food writer and chef with expertise spanning multiple culinary disciplines. With a passion for making home cooking accessible, she specializes in guiding readers through everything from hearty casseroles to delicate pastries. Her work is known for its clear instructions, practical tips, and deep understanding of both traditional and modern cooking techniques.